D1046845

| DATE | | | |
|---|---|---|---|
|  |  |  |  |
|  |  |  |  |
|  |  |  |  |
|  |  |  |  |
|  |  |  |  |
|  |  |  |  |
|  |  |  |  |
|  |  |  |  |
|  |  |  |  |
|  |  |  |  |
|  |  |  |  |

© THE BAKER & TAYLOR CO.

# Macroeconomic Activity and Income Inequality in the United States

**CONTEMPORARY STUDIES IN ECONOMIC AND FINANCIAL ANALYSIS, VOLUME 55**

*Editors:* Robert J. Thornton and J. Richard Aronson, *Lehigh University*

# CONTEMPORARY STUDIES IN ECONOMIC AND FINANCIAL ANALYSIS

*An International Seires of Monographs*

Series Editors: **Robert J. Thornton** and **J. Richard Aronson**

Lehigh University

# Macroeconomic Activity and Income Inequality in the United States

by   JOSEPH H. HASLAG
*Federal Reserve Bank of Dallas*
*Texas*

WILLIAM R. RUSSELL
DANIEL SLOTTJE
*Department of Economics*
*Southern Methodist University*

JAI PRESS INC.

*Greenwich, Connecticut*                    *London, England*

**Library of Congress Cataloging-in-Publication Data**

Slottje, Daniel.
   Macroeconomic activity and income inequality in the United States
   by Daniel Slottje, William R. Russell, Joseph H. Haslag.
      p.    cm.—(Contemporary studies in economic and financial
   analysis; v. 55)
   Bibliography: p.
   ISBN 1-55938-003-9
   1. United States—Economic policy—1945–  2. Income distribution–
   United States.   I. Russell, William R.   II. Haslag, Joseph H.
   III. Title.   IV. Series.
   HC106.5.S475   1989
   339.2′0973—dc20

*Copyright © 1989 JAI PRESS INC.*
*55 Old Post Road, No. 2*
*Greenwich, Connecticut 06830*

*JAI PRESS LTD.*
*3 Henrietta Street*
*London WC2E 8LU*
*England*

*ISBN: 1-55938-003-9*

*Library of Congress Catalog Card Number: 89-32429*

*Manufactured in the United States of America*

# CONTENTS

# List of Charts

*Chapter VII*

# List of Figures

***Chapter IV***

# List of Tables

**Chapter V.**

*Chapter VI.*

*Chapter VII.*

To
    Sara, Elizabeth, Stephen and Peter
                        J. H. H.
To
    Him, and to Cyma, Randi, Robert and Lon
                        W. R. R.
To
    Nana and Papa
                        D. J. S.

# Chapter I

# *Introduction*

The study of income distributions has concerned economists since the seminal work of Pareto almost one hundred years ago. The purpose of our current study is to examine the impact of macroeconomic activity, specifically, public policy actions, on the size distribution of total income and on the size distributions of various components of income in the United States. Public policymakers constantly face difficult alternatives as to which policy or mix of policies to implement. It is the aim of this study to provide these individuals with information as to how various policy mixes will affect macroeconomy and ultimately impact the size distribution of income.

Danziger, Haveman and Plotnick (1981) reviewed an extensive literature examining the effects of fiscal policy changes on the size distribution of income. For example, changes in tax policies and in transfer programs are postulated to have labor supply effects which, in turn, are transmitted into changes in the size distribution of earnings. Monetary policy actions, however, have received little attention although it is not unreasonable to suspect that Federal Reserve behavior has redistributional effects. For example, in a general equilibrium framework, the immediate effect of a money supply change is assumed to disturb the existing steady state equilibrium. With ensuing relative price changes during the adjustment to a new equilibrium, the money supply shock will result in quantity distortions in markets, which may give rise to redistributional consequences. The process just described involving linkages between monetary policy shocks and relative price changes, leading ultimately to changes in inequality which are not well understood. One aim of this current study is to explore this process. We do not neglect the redistributional consequences of fiscal policies—we simply do not exclude monetary policy effects. Therefore, a broader set of policy actions are considered as possible factors influencing the size distribution of income.

We divide our study into seven chapters. In Chapter II we present a broad overview of trends in policymaking, keeping an eye toward stated intentions as well as actions. The historical record of policy-maker's behavior indicates the primary reasons for taking a particular action.

Chapter III reviews some of the issues involved in income inequality. For example, to discuss the impact of policy decisions on inequality necessarily requires us to define what we mean by income and what we mean by inequality in the chosen measure of income. Different techniques and the problems inherent in measuring income inequality are discussed.

Chapter IV develops a general framework used throughout our analysis. Income components are assumed to be jointly distributed according to a particular hypothetical functional form. Existing data allow us to estimate the parameters of functional form, and hence the effects of policy actions on the income components. It is also possible to look at the changes in the size distribution of total income using the aforementioned hypothetical joint distribution. Prior to engaging in estimating the effects of policy actions, we investigate how relative price changes may affect the Gini coefficient derived from the statistical distribution as a measure of income inequality. We begin with relative price changes since it is likely that at least part of the transmission mechanism whereby money affects income distributions in the U.S. is through changes in relative prices caused by disequilibrium adjustments working through markets.

In Chapter V we analyze the impact of monetary and fiscal policy variables on income inequality from a static modelling approach. By undergoing a sensitivity analysis, information is provided as to how various policy combinations may actually impact the level of inequality.

Chapter VI extends the static analysis conducted in the previous chapter to a dynamical setting. We estimate (through elementary situations) how various policies will work through the economy over time to actually impact the size distribution of income.

Chapter VII focuses on the policy effects on the size distribution of several major income components, namely wage and salary income, interest income and dividend income.

# Chapter II

# *An Overview of Postwar Fiscal and Monetary Policy*

## I. INTRODUCTION

The set of "ultimate" goals set forth in the Employment Act of 1946 (hereafter "the Act") were designed to guide macroeconomic policy making. As listed in the Act, these goals are:

> free competitive enterprise and the general welfare, conditions under which there will be afforded useful employment opportunities, including self-employment, for those able, willing and seeking to work, and to promote maximum employment, production and purchasing power.[1]

The broad terminology used in the Act apparently served two purposes. First, the goals were not too specific in the sense of constricting policymakers to monitor particular economic variables.

Second, the Act did not intend to prioritize goals. Arthur Burns (1964) claimed "the moral commitment to full employment has been reaffirmed time and again by successive Presidents and successive Congresses."[2] However, it is not obvious that policymakers have exhibited the same attitude regarding the relative importance of stimulating economic activity versus other goals in their preference set. By simply enumerating policy goals, the Act does not suggest that full employment is more important than price stability, or vice versa. Consequently, the Act serves as a heuristic for policymakers to follow, allowing sufficient latitude to formulate policy based on relative preference weights.

The lack of preeminence among goals provides the policymaker with additional freedom. During much of the postwar era, policymakers have believed that at least a short-run trade-off between unemployment and inflation existed. This trade-off implies that policymakers are required to prioritize conflicting goals when formulating policy. To avoid such conflict in policymaking would require omniscience in the timing of policy actions.

In this chapter, we will provide an overview of major policymaking decisions since World War II. Quotes from the Economic Report of the President will be used extensively to infer the relative importance of price stability and stimulating economic activity in the policymaker's preference set. By doing so, the description of economic policy will provide a backdrop for the analysis of policy effects on the size distribution of income which is the purpose of this monograph.

## II. THE POSTWAR TRANSITION

With the end of hostilities in 1945, the federal government faced the challenge of transforming the wartime economy into a peacetime one. Obviously, the policymaker's objective was to make this conversion run as smoothly as possible. There were several major logistical considerations for decision-makers to overcome.

Plans to accommodate the influx of returning soldiers in the U.S. labor force was an important consideration. Gains in the labor force were expected to be partially offset by a large number of females returning to the home. However, uncertainty about the exact nature of the changes in the composition and the magnitude of the labor force posed a problem to policymakers. Timing was critical in implementing policy so as to minimize the effects of the labor market dynamics on the macroeconomy.

Overall in the commodity market, the combination of patriotic sentiment and shortages in consumer goods during the war had resulted in pent-up demand and liquidity. It was feared that this combination would put upward pressure on prices, particularly in light of the conversion time necessary to switch to the production of consumer items. Similar concerns about housing shortages led many to believe that rents would also rise in response to the increased demand associated with returning soldiers.

In response to postwar inflationary pressures, in 1945 President Truman requested extensions to the Emergency Price Control Act of 1942. Another extension was requested in 1946, however it was late July before the extensions were actually signed. With the 1945 extension elapsing on June 30, price controls were not in effect for a period of about one month. The absence of price controls suggests how effective this form of market intervention was. Wholesale prices increased at a 5 percent rate from January through June 1946. During July, however, wholesale prices increased at a 10 percent annual rate. Moreover, with price controls ending June 30, 1947, the 1947 inflation rate was 14.3 percent, whereas the rate of inflation recorded in 1948 was 7.7 percent. Hence, the price controls deferred underlying price increases until price controls were lifted rather than eliminate the upward pressure on prices.

The issue of rent controls was addressed in the Housing and Rent Act of 1947. The need for rent prices was identified by President Truman who stated that the supply of housing "was still radically out of balance with demand."[3] The hope was that rent controls would allow the supply of housing to catch up. Such controls were maintained in some form until mid-1951.

Beginning in November 1948 the U.S. economy experienced its first postwar recession. Lasting until October 1949, the recession was marked by a lack of new spending programs being introduced to combat the downswing. Immediately following the contraction was a period of rising prices. Prior to the beginning of the recession, Truman had indicated that inflation fighting was given top priority in his administration as indicated by his use of price controls and also by a proposed inflation reduction program announced in 1947. It is likely that Truman's inflation stance inhibited the introduction of new spending programs designed to mitigate the effects of the recession. However, the combination of the Tax Revenue Act of 1947 and increased unemployment compensation during the recession saw the federal budget surplus of $8.3 billion recorded in 1948 become a budget deficit of $2.6 billion in 1949. Thus, despite the fiscal nonaction during the 1948–1949 recession in the sense that no new spending programs were introduced, fiscal policy was viewed as being stimulative.

Perhaps the inactive fiscal response was more informative, because the recession was relatively short-lived, and the fiscal response suggested that activist fiscal policy was not necessary to end a contraction. Stein wrote "a passive fiscal policy, a policy of relying on the built-in responses of taxes and certain expenditures—notably unemployment compensation—to a recession when it occurs, seemed to come off well."[4] Indeed, the eleven month slowdown in economic activity was viewed as the strongest endorsement for the automatic stabilizers to date.

Monetary policy was being transformed during the period immediately following World War II. Pegging Treasury security prices was the apparent policy during the war. While this practice minimized debt servicing costs for the Treasury, monetization of government debt gives rise to faster reserve growth.

During the late 1940s and early 1950s, members of the (FOMC) became increasingly dissatisfied with the policy of supporting government bond prices. With the outbreak of the Korean War of 1950, the independence of Federal Reserve policy became more hotly debated. The FOMC wanted to follow a more restrictive course, while the Treasury wanted to reduce the interest burden of government debt. At a time of conflicting policy courses, the controversy had to be resolved. An agreement was reached between the Treasury and Federal Reserve which stated:

> The Treasury and the Federal Reserve System have reached full accord with respect to debt management and monetary policies to be pursued in furthering their common purpose to assure the successful financing of the Government's requirements and, at the same time, to minimize monetization of the public debt.[5]

With the 1951 Treasury-Federal Reserve Accord, monetary policy was no longer committed to security price pegging for the Treasury. The positive outcome coming from this agreement was that independent monetary policy could be coordinated with fiscal policy to affect economic performance. When looking at the Eisenhower Administration we will see how this coordination was utilized in formulating policy.

## III. FISCAL RESTRAINT AND THE BALANCED BUDGET

The first successful Republican presidential aspirant in twenty-years, Dwight D. Eisenhower, took office in 1953. The political rhetoric leading up to the election focused on the divergent future courses of fiscal policy under Democratic and Republican leadership. The Democrats claimed that a Republican administration would return to the misguided balanced budget policies adopted by Hoover regardless of the state of the economy. It was the balanced budget philosophy in the face of economic contraction that was held largely responsible for the severity and length of the Great Depression. To Democrats the lesson was clear, the federal government is responsible for the performance of the economy and only Democrats had shown a commitment to state contingent policies.

In 1952 the rate of inflation was measured at 2.2 percent. Although inflation was below rates observed immediately after the war, it was unacceptable in the eyes of the new president. As Stein noted: "The (Eisenhower) administration believed that the underlying problem of those years, and most of the time the current and overt problem, was inflation."[6]

In support of Stein's contention regarding the Eisenhower philosophy, the 1954 level of federal expenditures fell $7.3 billion. This decrease in expenditures was carried out despite a recession which began in July 1953 and lasted until August 1954. In fact, the budget deficit actually decreased between 1953 and 1954 by $1.1 billion, which suggests that the fiscal policy had tightened during the recession. Inflation slowed further from the gains made in 1953 when the rate fell below one percent.

Credit for the short duration of the 1953–1954 contraction was given to three factors. (1) Monetary policy had exhibited a timely strategy of loosening about the middle of 1953, roughly concomitant with the beginning of the recession. (2) Tax cuts for individuals were enacted in early 1953, and (3) the built-in stabilizers were also credited with shortening the recession. The 1953–54 contraction marked the first postwar effort to stimulate economic growth using coordinated and independent fiscal and monetary policies.

With the beginning of the expansion in late 1954, policy became more concerned with potential inflationary pressures. More restrictive fiscal and monetary policies were adopted to ease upward pressure on prices. Eisenhower postponed a tax rate reduction scheduled to go into effect in April 1955. Further, the Federal Reserve raised its discount rate to 2 1/4 percent.

Evidence of restrictive policies continued through the period 1955–1957. Reversing a trend that began in 1952, the 1955 federal budget had a surplus of $4 billion. A budget surplus was recorded in 1956 and 1957 as well. Despite fiscal restraint, the rate of inflation rose from −0.4 percent in 1955 to 3.6 percent in 1957. In 1956 and 1957, the unemployment was between 4 and 4.5 percent, with the 4 percent level commonly recognized as the level of "full unemployment."

Beginning in August 1957, the economy experienced another recession. Although the contraction only lasted until April 1958, the downturn was thought to be more severe than previous postwar recession because of the dramatic decreases observed in the economy. For instance, industrial production fell 6.5 percent and the level of unemployment increased from 2.5 to 5.2 million people during these 6 months. In contrast, the level of unemployment fell roughly 2.1 million between July 1953 and March 1954. In addition to a contracting economy, prices continued to rise throughout the recession. At an annual rate, prices rose roughly 2 percent between August and March.

In response to the contraction, monetary growth was faster during the last half of 1957, but policy abruptly tightened with the beginning of the new year. The tightening was probably due to the continued inflation problem exhibited during the contraction. With regard to fiscal policy, President Eisenhower decided not to reduce taxes as he had in the previous recession. Even a temporary tax cut was rejected on two grounds: (1) only permanent changes in disposable income affected consumption spending; and (2) a temporary tax cut could easily become a permanent change, which could adversely affect the fight against inflation during an expansion.

Despite evidence that was inconsistent with an inflation-output trade-off, the six months of positive correlation between these two variables was generally dismissed by policymakers. The boom and bust philosophy continued to be the dominant theme in policymaking. The clearest indication of this dismissal was observed at the beginning of the upswing. In 1958, the federal budget deficit was a peacetime record, $10.3 billion. By 1960, the federal government recorded a $3 billion surplus, achieved largely through slower growth in federal expenditures. Combined with a tightening of monetary policy beginning in 1959, the evidence suggests that policymakers waited for the expansion to be under way before beginning to reduce inflationary pressures inherent with an upswing.

Eisenhower's philosophy did not change throughout his eight year tenure. Balancing the federal budget was the cornerstone of this philosophy. Through two recessions, the president indicated that built-in responses giving rise to budget deficits were acceptable. However, during periods of expansion, fiscal policy was resolved to fight inflation and balance the budget.

## IV. LEADING UP TO THE 1964 TAX CUT

At the time of the Presidential inauguration in 1961, the unemployment rate was hovering around 7 percent as the U.S. economy was again experiencing a contraction. The short-lived recovery following the 1958 recession was interpreted by some as indicating that more fundamental economic problems existed. Though the set of fundamental economic problems were never specified, the new administration appeared to be more active. To combat the contraction under way, Kennedy enacted policies that increased government expenditures in addition to the added spending associated with higher unemployment compensation disbursements. Combined with the lower tax revenues and the 1961 federal deficit was reported at $3.9 billion. The notion of a balanced budget persisted as evidenced by the references to a proposed budget surplus in the 1962 Economic Report.

Monetary policy exhibited a more restrictive stance through the first half of 1960 and then expanded throughout 1961 to stimulate the economy. In reviewing monetary policy the 1963 Economic Report stated:

> While long-term rates rose by one-third in 1958–60, they changed little or

actually declined in 1961–62. And the money supply grew much more rapidly in the present expansion than in the preceding one.[7]

From the policies enacted in the early 1960s and the tone of statements issued regarding the course of future policy, one may infer that fighting inflation was less important to Kennedy. The policies indicated a greater willingness to actively stimulate economic policy. Moreover, there was not an immediate move to more restrictive policies concomitant with the reappearance of an expanding economy. Perhaps the fact that the average annual rate of inflation was only 1.2 percent for the period 1960–1964 contributed to the low priority given to inflationary pressures. But, the fact remains that it was not until 1963, more than two years after the expansion began, that the budget recorded a modest $300 million surplus.

During the early 1960s, the unemployment rate remained around 5 1/2 percent. This level was interpreted as being above the full-employment level. With unemployment above its full-employment level, the level of real output must also be below its full-employment potential. Although the economy was expanding, policymakers and academics voiced concern over the economic waste associated with an under-performing economy.

Applying the current tax rate schedule to the measure of full-employment output, and taking the level of federal expenditures, it was estimated that the federal budget was experiencing a budget surplus. With the low rate of inflation and the presence of excess capacity, the economic wastes were addressed claiming that fiscal policy was overly restrictive during the early 1960s.

Although not new, the full-employment federal budget became the measure of fiscal policy, and claims that real output was $50 million below its potential level, the administration requested a tax cut to further stimulate the economy. Three years into the current expansion, the 1964 tax cut was enacted. Table II.1 shows how 1964 fared relative to 1963. Real GNP rose $100 billion (5.3 percent) and consumption expenditures increased $62.2 billion (5.5 percent). Meanwhile, the rate of inflation rose from 1.2 percent in 1963 to 1.3 percent in 1964. From this evidence the existence of substantial excess capacity in the economy meant that additional stimulus to economic activity did not necessarily result in fanning inflationary fires.

*Table II.1.* A Cursory Look at the Effects
of the 1964 Tax Cut

|  | 1963 | 1964 |
|---|---|---|
| Real GNP (1982 = 100)[1] | 1873.3 | 1973.3 |
| Consumption | 1108.4 | 1170.6 |
| Investment | 307.1 | 325.9 |
| Net Exports[2] | (1.9) | 5.9 |
| Government Expenditures | 114.2 | 118.2 |
| Tax Revenues | 114.4 | 114.9 |
| Surplus[3] | .3 | (3.3) |
| Inflation Rate | 1.2 | 1.3 |
| (CPI 1967 = 100) |  |  |

1. *Billions of 1982 dollars*
2. *Figures in parenthesis denote negative values.*
3. *May not add due to rounding errors.*
   *Data are obtained from various issues of the Economic Report of the President.*

# V. VIET NAM AND INFLATION REVISITED

   With United States involvement in Southeast Asia escalating, the Johnson Administration saw fit to de-emphasize the elimination of economic waste as a top priority. Besides the economy appeared to be approaching full employment. Now the attention of policymakers turned toward inflationary pressures which appeared to be increasing. It was anticipated that as the economy neared its potential, upward pressure on prices would begin to appear. The moderate increase of 0.4 percentage points in the inflation rate between 1964 and 1965 was followed by a sizable increase of 1.2 percentage points the next year.

   Contrary to the Eisenhower coordination of fiscal and monetary policy to reduce inflationary pressures, Johnson sought additional expenditures to finance the Viet Nam War and social programs to reduce the level of economic disparity within the society. Both programs were carry-overs from the Kennedy Administration. Citing the need to reduce the apparent disparity among individuals, policies directly attempted to affect the distribution of income. During the postwar era, economic policy generally had focused on maintaining aggregate performance, believing economic well-being would follow (cf. Bronfenner, 1971). Combined with maintaining the tax rate schedule enacted in the 1964 tax cut, the budget went from a $500 million surplus in 1965 to a $13.2 billion deficit in 1967.

Monetary policy was called upon to restrain growing inflation, however, when the rate of inflation soared to 4.2 percent in 1968, the administration began to take action. In the 1968 Economic Report, it was stated that "High interest rates and tight money can restrain the economy. But the cost of monetary restraint is high and unfair, imposed on a single industry—homebuilding."[8] A more restrictive fiscal policy appeared in the form of a 10 percent tax surcharge. This action was partially responsible for lowering the budget deficit to $6 billion in 1968. Extending the surcharge through 1969 combined with a reduction in federal spending of $400 million resulted in a budget surplus of $8.4 billion in 1969. Clearly, excessive inflation would not be tolerated, particularly in an economy which had enjoyed a continuous expansion for the previous eight years.

Prior to his departure in early 1969, Johnson made several policy suggestions about appropriate inflation fighting policies. Policies to be avoided were also listed. For instance, too much restraint in fiscal and monetary policy may induce a recession. Price and wage controls were believed to defer inflationary pressures not diminish them. Also, the option of not acting was believed to have signaled to the financial markets that policymakers had given up fighting inflation. Such a signal would be disruptive to financial markets and endanger the economic expansion. It was believed that each of these policy paths carried too high a price tag to be considered as viable options.

Apparently, the Nixon Administration initially agreed with Johnson's suggestions. Fiscal restraint came in the form of a slowdown of growth in expenditures and avoiding a planned tax cut. Tighter monetary policy would give rise to higher interest rates, and slow down investment spending due to the high costs of borrowing. Although the rate of inflation increased during 1969 relative to 1968, the expansion that began in late 1960 finally came to an end in October 1969.

Citing widespread support for wage and price controls, the administration chose to forego Johnson's advice. Price controls were instituted in August 1971. In the *1971* Economic Report price controls were cited as the policy capable of making simultaneous progress with respect to all major domestic macroeconomic goals. In the Economic Report, it was claimed that the controls would lower inflation expectations, thereby lowering upward pressure on wage contracts and defusing the wage-price spiral. Combined with more expansionary fiscal and monetary policy, the expansion under way was expected to gain momentum during 1972, which was associated with higher employment.

The evidence provided suggests that progress was made with respect to output, employment and prices between 1971 and 1972. The rate of inflation fell from 4.3 percent to 3.3 percent, the lowest annual rate of inflation recorded since 1967. The real GNP grew 5.7 percent compared to 3.4 percent for the previous year, and the civilian unemployment rate fell to 5.6 percent. Relative to the recent challenges facing policymakers, 1972 provided some relief in the sense that the direction of changes in key variables were more favorable.

Performance in the inflation arena faltered in 1973. Several factors contributed to this outcome. First, price and wage controls moved into Phase III of the administration's plan. As Phase III ended in the middle of 1973, the rate of inflation began to pick up. Perhaps more crucial to the inflation outlook was the Arab oil embargo which saw substantial increases in oil prices occur late in 1973.

Although the economy continued to expand during 1973, the performance during 1974 was dismal. Fiscal policy was more restrictive in 1973 after several years of deficits exceeding $16 billion. The federal budget deficit grew from $5.6 billion in 1973 to $11.5 billion in 1974. Although the larger deficit indicated a more expansive fiscal policy, this deficit was smaller than projected at the beginning of the year. Unanticipated revenues were caused by the high rate of inflation, which was recorded at 12.2 percent for the year.

Monetary policy exhibited a similar restrictive posture in both 1973 and 1974. Growth of M1 in 1973 slowed to 6.1 percent compared to 7.7 percent recorded in 1972. The intention of policymakers in 1974 was to continue to slow the growth of the monetary aggregates so as to slow the growth in spending and hence abate inflationary pressures. For 1974 growth of M1 slowed to 5.1

percent. Slowing monetary growth did not have immediate effects on the rate of inflation as it soared to 11 percent.

The fiscal policy retained its expansionary posture in 1975; enacting the Tax Reduction Act of 1975, which carried an $8 billion rebate to individuals, lowered income tax withholdings by $12 billion, and was the primary means of stimulating economic activity employed by the government. The budget deficit soared to $69.5 billion, while the real GNP fell 1.2 percent for the year.

Inflation slowed to 9.1 percent during 1975. Money growth was mixed through the year, showing rapid growth during much of the first and second quarters and then declining roughly coincident with the beginning of the third quarter. Interest rates generally fell throughout the first half of the year and remained stable during the second half.

Policymakers attempted to achieve an elusive goal of long-run stabilization. With that objective in mind, the strategy appeared to involve achieving growth in the real GNP, and then turning attention to the inflation problem. The 1976 Economic Report stated: "The monetary authorities recognize that the present levels of output and employment are still very far from satisfactory."[9] Further, fiscal policy had exhibited expansionary practices during the previous year. However, in 1976 the Economic Report also stated that too fast growth in the money supply was not consistent with progress in reducing inflation. In this period of rising prices and declining economic activity, there was some indication that the government was attempting to make simultaneous progress on both fronts.

Industrial production showed strength during 1976, however gains in employment, reflected as changes in the unemployment rate, moderated. However, employment numbers exhibited strength. Hence, moderation in the unemployment rate figures implied that the labor force was growing at roughly the same rate as employment.

As a new administration took office, the economic recovery was strong, and some progress was made against inflation. Still economic reform was called for, largely to respond to accumulation of policies enacted to achieve social reform and affect economic performance. At this time many viewed the government as too intrusive in too many aspects of their lives. Evidence of excessive government was often as simple as the growing ratio of government purchases to real GNP. The question at hand was, how to achieve a larger private share of the economy without endangering the recovery?

## VI. THE INFLATION-OUTPUT CORRELATION

As Carter took office in 1977, the economy had continued to expand for nearly two years. Real output grew at a rate of 5 percent or better since the end of the 1974–1975 recession. Unemployment rates had fallen steadily to 6 percent by the year 1978. In his first Economic Report, the President called for prudent budget policies. The meaning of "prudent" is not immediately obvious. More specific references to the intention of fiscal policy involved reducing the deficit and the ratio of government spending to total demand. Both of these goals were to be achieved through judicious reform so as not to jeopardize the current expansion.

With this broad policy guideline in mind, the administration's resolve to maintaining the expansion was tested in 1978. Inflation accelerated during the year. Should the "boom and bust" philosophy of the past be reinstated or should the inflation be allowed to run its course. The administration's answer was: "We will not try to wring inflation out of economic system by pursuing policies designed to bring about a recession."[10] Growth in output did not slow appreciably during 1978, the GNP recorded a 5 percent increase, unfortunately, the rate of inflation accelerated to 9 percent for the year.

The combination of higher tax revenues, partially induced by the higher rates of inflation, and strong growth reduced the federal deficit to 29.5 billion in 1978. However, the high rate of inflation and continued deficit were considered too problematic. The relative importance of fighting inflation apparently usurped economic growth during 1979 as a top priority. With another oil price shock experience, consumer prices rose 13.3 percent during 1979. Moreover, the GNP growth slowed from 5 percent to 2.8 percent.

With a more tenuous outlook for continued expansion, the 1980 Economic Report called for more restrictive policy actions, specifically, reducing budget deficits achieved by "holding down Federal spending and foregoing tax reductions." Room for discretion in budgetary matters was claimed to be smaller due to current inflationary pressures. In light of the administration's stated policies, with the recession of 1980, the federal deficit rose from $16.1 billion in 1979 to $61.2 billion in 1980. Hence, the true resolve to fight inflation was not readily apparent from the fiscal policies undertaken. On the other hand, monetary policy showed a substantial tightening. The Federal Reserve stated a change in operating procedure beginning in October 1979, which focused on targeting reserves as opposed to the federal funds rate. Market interest rates began to rise and may well have further slowed the demand for investment goods.

## VII. SUMMARY

In summary, the evolution of fiscal and monetary policy has focused primarily on the development of two indicators of economic activity—the real GNP, and the price level. Fiscal policy actions are summarized over the period from 1946–1980 in Table II.2. As the table indicates, since 1958, the federal budget has recorded a budget surplus in 4 of the 23 periods in the sample. Prior to 1958, however, the federal budget recorded surpluses in 8 of the 12 years after the end of the war. Perhaps more indicative of the evolution of spending and receipts, the elements of the surplus, is a plot of the time path of growth rates in these variables. Using the data presented in Table II.2, Charts II.1 and II.2 graphically display this information. For both receipts and expenditures, the volatility appears to have *decreased* since the late 1950s, thus indicating that policy has actually been more stable. This observation, however, is inconsistent with the story that fiscal policy has exhibited a "boom and bust" philosophy over the postwar period.

Contrary to the more stable fiscal course, Table II.3 presents the year-to-year rates of inflation over the 1946–1980 period. By charting the rate of price change over time (see Chart II.3), there appears to be three distinct periods in the time path of the inflation rate. First, immediately following World War II, the rate of

*Table II.2.*  Federal Government Expenditures,
Revenues and Budget Surplus, National
Income and Product Accounts, 1946–80
(billions $)

| Year | Expenditures | Revenues | Surplus |
|------|-------------|----------|---------|
| 1946 | 35.6  | 39.1  |   3.5 |
| 1947 | 29.8  | 43.2  |  13.4 |
| 1948 | 34.9  | 43.2  |   8.3 |
| 1949 | 41.3  | 38.7  | − 2.6 |
| 1950 | 40.8  | 50.0  |   9.2 |
| 1951 | 57.8  | 64.3  |   6.5 |
| 1952 | 71.1  | 67.3  | − 3.7 |
| 1953 | 77.1  | 70.0  | − 7.1 |
| 1954 | 69.8  | 63.7  | − 6.0 |
| 1955 | 68.1  | 72.6  |   4.4 |
| 1956 | 71.9  | 78.0  |   6.1 |
| 1957 | 79.6  | 81.9  |   2.3 |
| 1958 | 88.9  | 78.7  | −10.3 |
| 1959 | 91.0  | 89.8  | − 1.1 |
| 1960 | 93.1  | 96.1  |   3.0 |
| 1961 | 101.9 | 98.1  | − 3.9 |
| 1962 | 110.4 | 106.2 | − 4.2 |
| 1963 | 114.2 | 114.4 |   0.3 |
| 1964 | 118.2 | 114.9 | − 3.3 |
| 1965 | 123.8 | 124.3 |   0.5 |
| 1966 | 143.6 | 141.8 | − 1.8 |
| 1967 | 163.7 | 150.5 | −13.2 |
| 1968 | 180.5 | 174.4 | − 6.0 |
| 1969 | 188.4 | 196.9 |   8.4 |
| 1970 | 204.3 | 191.9 | −12.4 |
| 1971 | 220.6 | 198.6 | −22.0 |
| 1972 | 244.3 | 227.5 | −16.8 |
| 1973 | 264.2 | 258.6 | − 5.6 |
| 1974 | 299.3 | 287.8 | −11.5 |
| 1975 | 356.6 | 287.3 | −69.3 |
| 1976 | 384.8 | 331.8 | −53.1 |
| 1977 | 421.1 | 375.2 | −45.9 |
| 1978 | 461.0 | 431.6 | −29.5 |
| 1979 | 509.7 | 493.6 | −16.1 |
| 1980 | 602.1 | 540.9 | −61.2 |

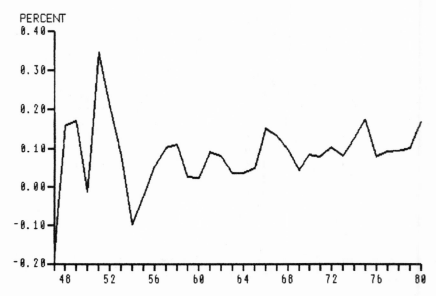

*Chart II.1.* Annual Growth Rates of Federal Expenditures.

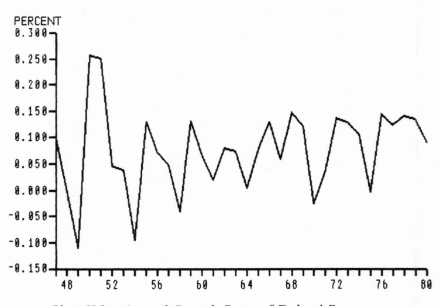

*Chart II.2.* Annual Growth Rates of Federal Revenues.

*Table II.3.* Rate of Change
in Consumer Prices and M1,
1946–1980

| Year | Inflation Rate | M1 Growth |
|------|----------------|-----------|
| 1946 | 8.5 | 39.1 |
| 1947 | 14.4 | 43.2 |
| 1948 | 7.8 | 43.2 |
| 1949 | −1.0 | 38.7 |
| 1950 | 1.0 | 50.0 |
| 1951 | 7.9 | 64.3 |
| 1952 | 2.2 | 67.3 |
| 1953 | 0.8 | 70.0 |
| 1954 | 0.5 | 63.7 |
| 1955 | −0.4 | 72.6 |
| 1956 | 1.5 | 78.0 |
| 1957 | 3.6 | 81.9 |
| 1958 | 2.7 | 78.7 |
| 1959 | 0.8 | 89.8 |
| 1960 | 1.6 | 0.6 |
| 1961 | 1.0 | 3.3 |
| 1962 | 1.1 | 1.8 |
| 1963 | 1.2 | 3.6 |
| 1964 | 1.3 | 4.5 |
| 1965 | 1.7 | 4.6 |
| 1966 | 2.9 | 2.4 |
| 1967 | 2.9 | 6.4 |
| 1968 | 4.2 | 7.4 |
| 1969 | 5.4 | 3.2 |
| 1970 | 5.9 | 5.1 |
| 1971 | 4.3 | 6.3 |
| 1972 | 3.3 | 8.8 |
| 1973 | 6.2 | 5.4 |
| 1974 | 11.0 | 4.3 |
| 1975 | 9.1 | 4.8 |
| 1976 | 5.8 | 6.4 |
| 1977 | 6.5 | 7.7 |
| 1978 | 7.7 | 7.9 |
| 1979 | 11.3 | 6.9 |
| 1980 | 13.5 | 6.4 |

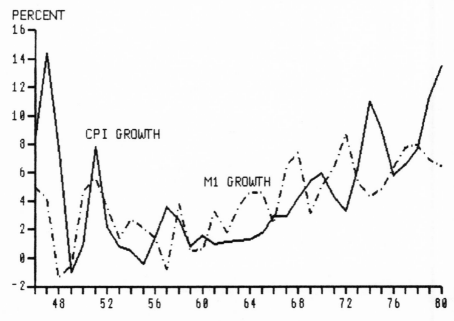

*Chart II.3.* Annual Growth Rates of Consumer Prices and M1.

inflation, as measured by the CPI, was extremely volatile. Beginning in the early 1950s, the fluctuations in the inflation became smaller with a slight upward trend surfacing in the 1960s. Toward the end of the 1960s, the rate of ascent in the inflation measure became more steep. Moreover, the amplitude of the inflation rate cycle appears to have grown following the period of relative tranquility in the rate of price increase referred to above.

Also reported in the same table is the annual growth rate of M1. The reader can see from Chart II.3 that a faster rate of growth in the money supply generally preceded a higher rate of inflation. The time between peaks in the rate of monetary growth and the rate of inflation, however, were highly variable. Moreover, contrary to decreasing amplitude in the cycle of federal expenditures and revenues, money growth appears to exhibit greater amplitude in a series that also is trending upward.

Meanwhile, inflation rates seem to break into three distinct time frames. First, following the war until the late-1950s the rate of price increase was exhibiting "damped cycle" behavior. Beginning in the 1960s, the inflation followed a stable growth path trending upward over the decade. The 1970s saw a return in variability in the inflation rate, with the cycle appearing explosive rather than dampening as was observed in the immediate postwar period.

Throughout much of the postwar era, the dominant policy philosophy, at least spoken, hinged on the existence of a Phillips curve trade-off between unemployment and inflation. Yet several periods during the 1946–1980 era, a positive correlation existed between these key economic variables. The first postwar experience of this positive correlation was dismissed as an anomaly. Subsequent experiences during the 1970s provided interesting test cases for policymakers in setting priorities. Policymakers tended to vacillate, resulting in uncoordinated policy actions.

In undergoing many fiscal and monetary policy actions from 1945–1981, the federal government showed great concern about unemployment and inflation and little concern about the redistribution consequences of such actions. Exceptions, of course, were Kennedy's New Frontier and Johnson's Great Society programs of the mid-1960s. In the rest of this book we present an analysis which attempts to clarify the mechanism(s) whereby these policies do impact the observed level of economic inequality.

## NOTES

1.  79th U.S. Congress, Full Employment Act of 1946
2.  Arthur Burns, The Condition of the American Economy, American Enterprise Institute
3.  *Congressional Quarterly*, 1946–64, pg. 811.
4.  Herbert Stein, *The Fiscal Revolution in America*, University of Chicago Press, 1969, pg. 239.
5.  *The Federal Reserve Bulletin*, March 1951, pg. 267.
6.  Stein, *The Fiscal Revolution in America*, pg. 283.
7.  *The Economic Report of the President*, Council of Economic Advisors, Government Printing Office, 1963, pg. 6.
8.  *The Economic Report of the President*, Council of Economic Advisors, Government Printing Office, 1968, pg. 10.
9.  *The Economic Report of the President*, Council of Economic Advisors, Government Printing Office, 1976, pg. 21.
10.  *The Economic Report of the President*, Council of Economic Advisors, Government Printing Office, 1978, pg. 7.

# Chapter III

# *Measuring Economic Inequality*

## I. INTRODUCTION

Numerous models and measures have been proffered to explain
and measure inequality in the personal multivariate distribution
of income.

The problem of inequality in the distribution of income in a
given society has concerned economists and public policy makers
for a long time. As Kakwani notes, "The phenomenon of income
inequality has been a source of worldwide social upheaval. It has
become a weapon in the hands of social reformers and a point of
intellectual debate among academics" (Kakwani 1980, p. 3). Many
partial and ad hoc theories have been developed in the past. Recently, Sahota (1978) surveyed the personal income distribution
literature with excellent detailed summaries of the existing body
of theoretical work. Sahota groups the various theories into two
basic categories:

(a) theories that are based on the belief that people can make their own
fate and societies can mold significantly the relative income positions of
their members, and (b) theories that convey the gospel that inequalities are
largely preordained. The first group ranges from the 'choice' theories of
the conservative economists who believe that income inequalities are
largely a consequence of voluntary choice to the inheritance, and institu-
tional theories of liberal and radical economists who hold that inequalities
can be reduced, but only by changing the social order. In the fatalist (b)
group, one may distinguish three schools: (b₁) the theories anchored on
the premise that abilities, as the main determinant of earning differences,

25

are genetically determined; (b₂) the theories that postulate that inequalities are caused largely by unmanipulatable chance, luck, and stochastic factors; and (b₃) the life-cycle theories, according to which a substantial degree of income inequality at any point in time is inevitable due to the sheer age effect on earning capacities (however determined) (Sahota 1978, p. 2).

The first category that Sahota mentions arises from three subgroups or schools of thought. The first group is represented by such scholars as Mincer (1958, 1970, 1974), T. W. Schultz (1963), T. P. Schultz (1965), Becker (1962, 1967) and Chiswick (1974). It has been criticized for only being concerned with the supply side of the market for production factors, essentially labor with various levels of training and education. The second group of scholars focus their attention on the demand side of the market, and the demand for different types of labor. These models are derived from production functions that include different types of labor. The representative scholars of this group include Bowles (1969), Dougherty (1971, 1972), and Psacharopoulos and Hinchliffe (1972). The third group considers income distribution a consequence of the supply and demand for various kinds of labor. Tinbergen (1975) is the chief proponent of this school. His analysis consists of not only labor income, but also incomes from other factors of production.

## II. REVIEW OF THE THEORETICAL LITERATURE

Based on chronological order and on the close relationships between the various schools of thought, Sahota rearranged the previous theoretical groups into nine classes.

### A. Ability Theory

According to the ability theory, differences in workers' productivity and their earnings were due to differences in abilities (cf. Galton, 1869). Abilities were thought to be normally distributed. Pareto (1897) took umbrage with this theory when he discovered that incomes are better described by a lognormal distribution with a flat upper tail that implies a substantial unequal distribution of income. Pigou (1932) theorized that the discrepancy between the distribution of abilities and incomes was due to two things: (1) a skewed distribution of inherited wealth, and (2) the existence of what he referred to as "noncompeting groups." Mincer (1970, 1976) and Becker (1967) developed explanations similar to Pigou's, replacing "innate ability" with "acquired human capital" as the source of embodiment.

## B. Stochastic Theory

As Sahota (1978) notes, the stochastic theory is one of the oldest and most crucial theories of distribution. Theorists in this group believed that the skewed shape of income distribution was a function of chance, luck, and random occurrences. Underlying this theory is the notion that even if all individuals income and wealth began with perfect equality, the inequalities described by the Pareto distribution could occur simply because of stochastic forces acting over time (cf. Creedy, 1985).

## C. Individual Choice Theory

The individual choice theory by Friedman (1953) describes an optimizing model of income differences. This is the precursor of modern human capital theory. Individual choices among various opportunities are determined by expectations of future pecuniary and nonpecuniary returns over time. The different attitudes of people towards risk depend on their incomes. The distribution of risk preferences influences not only the income differential between risk-lovers and risk-avoiders, but also the direction of skewedness of incomes. Dynamic societies have many more risk-avoiders than risk-lovers. Thus, a substantial portion of income inequality is due to initial differences in endowments of property and human capacity. This view distinguishes Friedman's theory from present day human capital theory.

## D. Human Capital Theory

The human capital approach attempts to explain the structure of incomes by individual investment in education and on-the-job training. This theory maintains that investment in human capital is the result of a rational optimization decision based on the discounted present value of alternative life cycle income streams.

More generally, human capital theory is a generalization of standard capital theory applied to human investments of a different nature (cf. T. W. Schultz, 1963).

### E. Theories of Educational Inequalities

As Sahota (1978) points out, these theories started with the 1954 Supreme Court decision that "separate but equal" educational facilities produced unequal results. From this ruling, came a search by educators for the determinants of educability. Before 1960, the determinants of educability were thought to be the general socioeconomic status and intelligence of students. Hunt (1961) theorized and validated the view that educability is based on the environment of the student given the genetically predetermined physical limitation. Also Schultz (1963) analyzed the economic effects of education using a human capital approach. It was from these studies that Project Head Start, school lunch programs, and other increased school resources for the poor came about.

### F. Inheritance Theory

Empirical findings indicate that nonlabor income distribution is more unequally distributed than earned incomes. The major source of this inequity is inheritance. Hence, inheritance theory should be addressed in an analysis of income distribution. "According to this theory, capitalists perpetuate their economic positions: the more they have, the more they invest and accumulate, the more profits they earn, the more they can save and reinvest, the more capital gains they receive, so the spiral goes on" (Sahota 1978, p. 22). This model did not hold up, however, under empirical testing. Empirical research supports the view that factor shares do not necessarily correspond with rich and poor classes, investment encompasses more than just capitalists' savings, mobility between classes is significant, and property rights are less well defined as countries become wealthier (cf. Lydall, 1968).

It is true, however, that property income is still a significant component of personal income, especially for the rich. Wealth tends to multiply with other characteristics, like education and acquired abilities.

## G. Life Cycle Theory

The life-cycle theory states that an individual's income increases with age initially, and then decreases as the aging process continues toward retirement thus conforming to an inverted parabola. A life cycle of income is actually a more appropriate measure for analyzing inequalities than income at a point in time simply because income inequalities will be overstated when measured at a point in time (cf. Cowell, 1977; Creedy, 1985).

## H. Public Income Distribution Theories

Public income includes the provision of public goods, services, and transfer payments. As Sahota (1978) notes, public sectors in modern economies play a fairly important role. For instance, individuals' choice among changes, their desires and incentives to take risks, to work, to save, and to invest are influenced to varying extents by various taxes, public expenditures, transfer payments, and public regulation of economic activities. Therefore, to design a fair economic society is to design a tax and income reward system. Evidently, "the theory of public income distribution ought to form an integral part of any comprehensive theory of distribution" (Sahota 1978, p. 28). One conclusion of this theory is that public income is distributed more equally than is private income. Inequalities and productivity decrease as the public sector increases.

## I. Theories of Distributive Justice

The theory of distributive justice, from the viewpoint of positive economics, explains "why income distribution has come to be what it is and how the distribution is predicted to change in the future" (Sahota 1978, p. 34). Hobbs, Locke and other seventeenth century natural law philosophers felt all people have the right to the fruits of their labor. With several factors of production one can wonder who the real producer is, and who should claim these fruits. Traditional economics support marginal productivity theory which divides the fruits based on skill and endowments. As has been noted, however, neither the ownership of capital nor innate ability are distributed equally.

None of the previously mentioned theories are considered to be a general theory. All of them can only be called partial theories of personal income distribution. These partial theories each clarify one link in the distribution question. Unfortunately we cannot take a convex combination and create a more general theory.

## III. REVIEW OF THE EMPIRICAL LITERATURE

Historically, little data have existed to undergo rigorous empirical testing. Recently, however, access to longitudinal data has allowed researchers to start reducing the gap between pure theory and measurable variates.

All of the aforementioned theories are concerned with how the observed personal income distribution is actually generated. Measuring the personal income distribution and attendant inequality is another matter. As Sen (1973) points out, measures of inequality can be divided into normative and positive categories. The normative measures are concerned with measuring inequality in terms of the social welfare content so that a higher degree of inequality corresponds to a lower level of social welfare for a given total of income. Among the normative measures, Dalton's (1920) measure is best known. Dalton based his measure on the sum of individual utilities. His measure is based on a comparison between actual levels of aggregate utility, and the level of total utility that would obtain if income were equally divided. Dalton took the ratio of actual social welfare to the maximal social welfare as his measure of equality. Atkinson (1970) noted that Dalton's measure is not invariant to positive linear transformations of the utility function; his measure implies cardinal utility which means any positive linear transformation would do just as well, so Dalton's measure takes arbitrary values depending on which particular transformation is chosen. Atkinson's own approach is to redefine the measure in such a way that the actual numbers used in measuring would be invariant with respect to permitted transformations of the welfare numbers. Atkinson defines what he calls "the equally distributed equivalent income" of a given distribution of total income, and this is defined as that level of per capita income which, if enjoyed by everybody, would make total welfare exactly equal to the total welfare generated by the actual income distribution. Putting $y_e$ as "the equally distributed equivalent income," we see that:

$$y_e = y \;\Big|\; \Big[\; nU(y) = \sum_{i=1}^{n} U(y_i) \;\Big]. \tag{3.1}$$

The sum of the actual welfare levels of all individuals equals the welfare sum that would emerge if everyone had $y_e$ income. Since each $U(y)$ is taken to be concave, $y_e$ cannot be larger than the mean income $\mu$. Further, it can be shown that the more equal the distribution the closer will $y_e$ be to $\mu$. Atkinson's measure of inequality is:

$$A = 1 - \Big( \frac{y_e}{\mu} \Big). \tag{3.2}$$

If income is equally distributed then $y_e$ is equal to $\mu$, and the value of Atkinson's measure will be 0. The most obvious problem with this measure is that it is totally dependent on the form of the welfare function. Also, of course, the values of $U$ of each person are simply added together to arrive at aggregate social welfare. The aggregation problems involved with this simple sum approach to social welfare are well-known.

The measures which will now be described are positive measures in the sense that they make no explicit use of any concept of social welfare. The measures we now discuss follow Sen (1973). The first measure to be described is the range. Consider distributions of income over $n$ persons, $i = 1, \ldots, n$, and let $y_i$ be the income of person $i$. Let the average level of income be $\mu$, so that:

$$\sum_{i=1}^{n} y_i = n\,\mu. \tag{3.3}$$

The relative share of income going to person $i$ is $x_i$. That is:

$$y_i = n\,\mu x_i, \tag{3.4}$$

so the range measure is based on comparing the extreme values of the distribution, i.e., the highest and the lowest income levels. The range can be defined as the gap between these two levels as a ratio of mean income. The range $E$ is defined by:

$$E = \frac{(\text{Max}_i\, y_i - \text{Min}_i\, y_i)}{\mu}. \tag{3.5}$$

If income is divided absolutely equally, then $E = 0$. If one person receives all the income, then $E = n$. The problem with the range is that it ignores the distribution in between the extremes. A measure that examines the entire distribution is the relative mean deviation. This measure compares the income level of each individual with the mean income, to sum the absolute values of all the differences, and then to look at that sum as a proportion of total income. The relative mean deviation takes the form:

$$M = \frac{\sum_{i=1}^{n} |\mu - y_i|}{n \, \mu}.$$

(3.6)

With perfect equality $M = 0$ and with all income going to one person, $M = 2(n - 1)/n$. The major flaw with the relative mean deviation is that it is not sensitive to transfers from a poorer person to a richer person as long as both lie on the same side of the mean income. A very common statistical measure of the variation is the variance:

$$V = \frac{\sum_{i=1}^{n} (\mu - y_i)^2}{n}.$$

(3.7)

The problem with looking at the variance is that it depends on the mean income level, and one distribution may show much greater relative variation than another and still end up having a lower variance if the mean income level around which the variation takes place is smaller than the other distribution. A measure that doesn't have this deficiency and concentrates on relative variation is the coefficient of variation, which is simply the square root of the variance divided by the mean income level:

$$C = \frac{V^{1/2}}{\mu}.$$

(3.8)

A question that arises with the coefficient of variation asks whether it is best to measure the difference of each income level from the mean only, or should the comparison be carried out between every pair of incomes? By utilizing pairwise comparisons, everyone's income difference from everyone else's is taken into account. The standard deviation of logarithms is a measure of inequality that eliminates the arbitrariness of the units and therefore of absolute levels, since a change of units, which takes the form a multiplication of the absolute values, comes out in the logarithmic form as an addition of a constant, and therefore disappears when pairwise differences are being taken. The standard deviation of the logarithm takes the form:

$$H = \left[ \sum_{i=1}^{n} \frac{(\log \mu - \log y_i)^2}{n} \right]^{1/2} \tag{3.9}$$

The $H$ measure depends on the arbitrary squaring formula and shares with the variance and coefficient of variation the limitation of taking differences only from the mean.

A measure of economic inequality that has been widely used is the Gini coefficient attributed to Gini (1912). The Gini measure may be viewed in terms of the Lorenz curve. The Lorenz curve was devised by Lorenz (1905), whereby the percentages of the population arranged from the poorest to the richest are represented on the horizontal axis and the percentages of income enjoyed by the bottom $x$ percent of the population is shown on the vertical axis. A Lorenz curve runs from one corner of the unit square to the diametrically opposite corner. If everyone has the same income, the Lorenz curve is simply the diagonal. If bottom income groups have a proportionately lower share of income, the Lorenz curve will obviously lie below the diagonal. The Gini coefficient is the ratio of the difference between the line of absolute equality (the diagonal) and the Lorenz curve—to the triangle underneath the diagonal. The Gini coefficient may be defined as exactly one half of the relative mean difference, which is defined as the arithmetic average of the absolute values of differences between all pairs of incomes. From Sen (1973),

$$G = \left( \frac{1}{2} n^2 \mu \right) \sum_{i=1}^{n} \sum_{j=1}^{n} |y_i - y_j| \tag{3.10a}$$

$$= 1 - \left( \frac{1}{n^2} \right)_\mu \sum_{i=1}^{n} \sum_{i=j}^{n} \text{Min} \, (y_i, y_j) \tag{3.10b}$$

$$= 1 + \left( \frac{1}{2} \right) - \left( \frac{2}{n^2} \right)_\mu [y_1 + 2y_2 + \ldots + ny_n] \qquad (3.10c)$$

for $y_1 \geq y_2 \geq y_3 \ldots \geq y_n$.

Notice that the Gini avoids the total concentration on differences vis-à-vis the mean which $C$, $V$, or $H$ has. It also avoids the squaring procedures of $C$, $V$, and $H$. But the most appealing property of the Gini is that it looks at differences between every pair of incomes.

Another interesting measure of inequality, proposed by Theil (1967), comes from the notion of entropy in information theory.[1] Let $x$ be the probability that a certain event will occur, the information content $h(x)$ of noticing that the event has in fact occurred is a decreasing function of $x$—the more unlikely an event, the more interesting it is to know that the thing has really happened. Theil considered one case of this,

$$h(x) = \log \left( \tfrac{1}{x} \right). \qquad (3.11)$$

When there are $n$ possible events $1, \ldots, n$, we take the respective probabilities $x_1, \ldots, x_n$ such that $x_i \geq 0$ and $\sum_{i=1}^{n} x_i = 1$. The entropy or the expected information content of the situation can be viewed as the sum of the information content of each event weighted by the respective probabilities.

$$H(x) = \sum_{i=1}^{n} x_i h(x_i) \qquad (3.12a)$$

$$= \sum_{i=1}^{n} x_i \log \left( \frac{1}{x_i} \right) \qquad (3.12b)$$

The closer the $n$ probabilities $x_i$ are to $\left( \tfrac{1}{n} \right)$, the greater is the entropy. Interpreting $x_i$ as the share of income belonging to the $i$th individual, $H(x)$ is a measure of equality. When each $x_i$ equals $\tfrac{1}{n}$, $H(x)$ attains its maximum value of $\log n$. To get the index of inequality, we subtract the entropy $H(x)$ of an income distribution from its maximum value of $\log n$, we get an index of inequality. Theil's measure is then

$$T = log\ n - H(x) \qquad (3.13a)$$

$$= \sum_{i=1}^{n} x_i \log nx_i \qquad (3.13b)$$

The problem remains, however, that Theil's formula is arbitrary and, as Sen (1973) points out, taking the average of the logarithms of the reciprocals of income shares, weighted by income shares, is not a measure that is exactly overflowing with intuitive sense.

Many other lesser known measures do exist. Elteto and Frigyes (1968) proposed a measure that is based on relative mean deviation. Kakwani (1980) created a measure that utilizes the Lorenz curve and is sensitive to income transfers. Basmann and Slottje (1987) have invented a measure of inequality that promises to be more sensitive than the Gini ratio to changes in the economic distress suffered by the poor. All of these measures yield information on the inequality present in a given distribution. To rank one over another is meaningless because they measure different aspects of the given distribution. In this book, primary focus is on the Gini ratio. The Gini measure will be used to examine inequality in the income distribution. The Gini measure is used because it is mathematically convenient and satisfies most criteria of what an inequality measure should measure (cf. Champernowne, 1974).

Finally the choice of an appropriate hypothetical distribution to approximate the empirical distribution of income will be discussed. As was noted earlier, theories of how a particular income distribution was generated can be traced as far back as Smith. Pareto (1897), however, was one of the first individuals to actually hypothesize the size distribution of income and then to actually see how well it fit the empirical distribution. Unfortunately, Pareto's distribution has been found to do very poorly in fitting the overall empirical distribution but, does fit well at the tail ends of the distribution.[2] The lognormal distribution was also discussed previously as a hypothetical distribution and has been extensively examined by Aitchison and Brown (1969). They found that the lognormal form fit most of the income distribution well but did poorly at the tails. Numerous other probability density functions have been proposed as models of income distribution. Champernowne (1952) suggested a hypothetical distribution function but, as Fisk (1961) pointed out, it had systematic divergences from the empirical distribution. Fisk (1961) took a special case of Champernowne's distribution, the so-called Sech² distribution, and found it useful in comparing the distribution of groups of income units that are homogeneous in one characteristic—in Fisk's case, occupation. Amoroso (1925) first applied the gamma density to confront income data; they found the gamma to fit much better than the lognormal. Singh and Maddala (1976) obtained a function which is a generalization of the Pareto, Weibull, and Sech² distribution considered by Fisk (1961). Singh and Maddala estimated the parameters of a derived function for 1960–1972 family income data and concluded that the derived function provides a better fit to the data than either the gamma or lognormal forms. Discovery by McDonald and Ransom (1979) of inconsistencies in Singh and Maddala's parameter estimates puts the validity of the Singh-Maddala conclusions in question. Thurow (1970) first used the beta density function as a model for the distribution of income. McDonald and Ransom (1979) compared the beta density function to the lognormal, gamma, and Singh-Maddala functions as descriptive models for the distribution of family income for 1960 and 1969 through 1975. McDonald and Ransom recognized that the gamma is a limiting case of the beta. By deriving the Gini ratio for the four different functional forms they concluded that the beta density and Singh-Maddala density fit better than the lognormal density or gamma density. One frequently encountered problem with these comparisons, however, is that different estimation techniques are used to estimate the parameters of the different functions. Thus, McDonald and Ransom were cautious to conclude that the beta density fit better or vice versa because the performance of the two depended on the estimation technique. In another study, McDonald (1984) has demonstrated that a generalized beta density of the second kind fits income data better than the Singh-Maddala density, a generalized gamma density or the beta density of the first kind. It should be noted that all of the preceding discussion on theories of income distribution generation, measures of inequality in a given distribution and the choice of an appropriate model of the income distribution are concerned with the distribution of total income only. Below we discuss a new comprehensive approach to analyzing these questions.

# IV. CURRENT TRENDS IN INCOME INEQUALITY IN THE UNITED STATES

We conclude this chapter with a brief discussion of actual inequality levels in the United States for the 1947–1984 period. To analyze this question we utilize two different measures of inequality, quintiles of income earners from the *Current Population Reports* (CPR), and several summary inequality measures that we discussed above in Section III. We present the quintiles of income earners first. The CPR data are collected without adjusting for income in-kind and taxes paid although it does include cash transfers. It is for this reason that we utilize Internal Revenue Service data below in undergoing most of our analysis. We briefly report the CPR data results here, however, since that data set is in quintiles and allows us to explicitly track the level of inequality "from the data" as we now demonstrate. We will also present the Relative Mean Deviation (RMD), Gini coefficient (G), Kakwani measure (K) and Theil's entropy measure (T); all derived from the CPR quintile data.

As can be seen in Table III.1, the poorest 20 percent of income earners maintained a relatively stable (and tragic) 5 percent of total income over the 1947–1984 period. The so-called "Great Society" programs of the mid-1960s did not appear to have much impact on this groups share of the pie. Also evident from Table III.1 is the fact that the poorest (relatively speaking) 60 percent of the population accounted for approximately 33 percent of total income for the 1947–1984 period. The richest 40 percent of income earners thus controlled about two-thirds of income over this period and the richest 20 percent of income earners controlled roughly 43 percent of income over this period. A perusal of Chart III.1 indicates that the amount of income in each quintile has been relatively stable for the nearly 40 year period as well. The information in Table III.1 and Chart III.1 translates into the summary results given in Table III.2 and in Chart III.2. As can be seen, The Gini coefficient has a relatively stable measure of .41, recalling that a measure of 0 indicates perfect equality and 1 indicates perfect inequality. The other 3 summary measures also indicate very stable levels over the 40 year period.

We can summarize this section by noting then, that the level of

*Table III.1.* Quintile Data from the Current Population
Survey Series

| Year | Q1 | Q2 | Q3 | Q4 | Q5 |
|------|------|------|------|------|------|
| 1947 | 0.050 | 0.119 | 0.170 | 0.231 | 0.430 |
| 1948 | 0.049 | 0.121 | 0.173 | 0.232 | 0.424 |
| 1949 | 0.045 | 0.119 | 0.173 | 0.235 | 0.427 |
| 1950 | 0.045 | 0.120 | 0.174 | 0.234 | 0.427 |
| 1951 | 0.050 | 0.124 | 0.176 | 0.234 | 0.416 |
| 1952 | 0.049 | 0.123 | 0.174 | 0.234 | 0.419 |
| 1953 | 0.047 | 0.125 | 0.180 | 0.239 | 0.409 |
| 1954 | 0.045 | 0.121 | 0.177 | 0.239 | 0.418 |
| 1955 | 0.048 | 0.123 | 0.178 | 0.237 | 0.413 |
| 1956 | 0.050 | 0.125 | 0.179 | 0.237 | 0.410 |
| 1957 | 0.051 | 0.127 | 0.181 | 0.238 | 0.404 |
| 1958 | 0.050 | 0.125 | 0.180 | 0.239 | 0.407 |
| 1959 | 0.049 | 0.123 | 0.179 | 0.238 | 0.411 |
| 1960 | 0.048 | 0.122 | 0.178 | 0.240 | 0.413 |
| 1961 | 0.047 | 0.119 | 0.175 | 0.238 | 0.422 |
| 1962 | 0.050 | 0.121 | 0.176 | 0.240 | 0.413 |
| 1963 | 0.050 | 0.121 | 0.177 | 0.240 | 0.412 |
| 1964 | 0.051 | 0.120 | 0.177 | 0.240 | 0.412 |
| 1965 | 0.052 | 0.122 | 0.178 | 0.239 | 0.409 |
| 1966 | 0.056 | 0.124 | 0.178 | 0.238 | 0.405 |
| 1967 | 0.055 | 0.124 | 0.179 | 0.239 | 0.404 |
| 1968 | 0.056 | 0.124 | 0.177 | 0.237 | 0.405 |
| 1969 | 0.056 | 0.124 | 0.177 | 0.237 | 0.406 |
| 1970 | 0.054 | 0.122 | 0.176 | 0.238 | 0.409 |
| 1971 | 0.055 | 0.120 | 0.176 | 0.238 | 0.411 |
| 1972 | 0.054 | 0.119 | 0.175 | 0.239 | 0.414 |
| 1973 | 0.055 | 0.119 | 0.175 | 0.240 | 0.411 |
| 1974 | 0.055 | 0.120 | 0.175 | 0.240 | 0.410 |
| 1975 | 0.054 | 0.118 | 0.176 | 0.241 | 0.411 |
| 1976 | 0.054 | 0.118 | 0.176 | 0.241 | 0.411 |
| 1977 | 0.052 | 0.116 | 0.175 | 0.242 | 0.415 |
| 1978 | 0.052 | 0.116 | 0.175 | 0.241 | 0.415 |
| 1979 | 0.052 | 0.116 | 0.175 | 0.241 | 0.417 |
| 1980 | 0.051 | 0.116 | 0.175 | 0.243 | 0.416 |
| 1981 | 0.050 | 0.113 | 0.174 | 0.244 | 0.419 |
| 1982 | 0.047 | 0.112 | 0.170 | 0.243 | 0.427 |
| 1983 | 0.047 | 0.111 | 0.171 | 0.243 | 0.428 |
| 1984 | 0.047 | 0.110 | 0.170 | 0.244 | 0.429 |

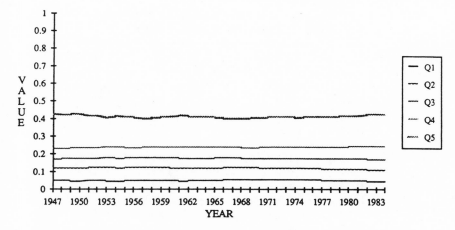

*Chart III.1.* Plot of Quintile Data for the U.S. 1947–1984

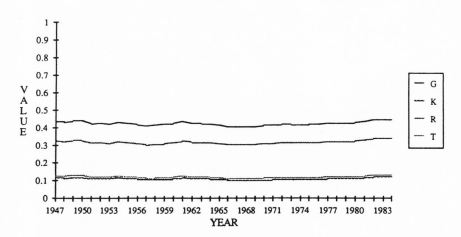

*Chart III.2.* Plot of Popular Income Inequality Measures for the U.S. 1947–1984

*Table III.2.*  Income Inequality Measures
for the U.S. 1947–1984

| Year | G | K | R | T |
|------|-------|-------|-------|-------|
| 1947 | 0.436 | 0.114 | 0.326 | 0.127 |
| 1948 | 0.432 | 0.111 | 0.321 | 0.124 |
| 1949 | 0.441 | 0.116 | 0.328 | 0.130 |
| 1950 | 0.439 | 0.117 | 0.326 | 0.129 |
| 1951 | 0.421 | 0.108 | 0.313 | 0.118 |
| 1952 | 0.427 | 0.109 | 0.317 | 0.121 |
| 1953 | 0.419 | 0.108 | 0.310 | 0.118 |
| 1954 | 0.432 | 0.114 | 0.321 | 0.125 |
| 1955 | 0.423 | 0.108 | 0.313 | 0.119 |
| 1956 | 0.415 | 0.107 | 0.308 | 0.115 |
| 1957 | 0.408 | 0.103 | 0.302 | 0.111 |
| 1958 | 0.413 | 0.106 | 0.307 | 0.114 |
| 1959 | 0.420 | 0.107 | 0.311 | 0.117 |
| 1960 | 0.423 | 0.111 | 0.316 | 0.119 |
| 1961 | 0.434 | 0.115 | 0.324 | 0.125 |
| 1962 | 0.423 | 0.108 | 0.316 | 0.118 |
| 1963 | 0.422 | 0.108 | 0.315 | 0.118 |
| 1964 | 0.421 | 0.107 | 0.315 | 0.117 |
| 1965 | 0.416 | 0.105 | 0.310 | 0.114 |
| 1966 | 0.405 | 0.101 | 0.303 | 0.108 |
| 1967 | 0.406 | 0.101 | 0.303 | 0.109 |
| 1968 | 0.407 | 0.098 | 0.303 | 0.109 |
| 1969 | 0.407 | 0.100 | 0.304 | 0.109 |
| 1970 | 0.414 | 0.102 | 0.309 | 0.113 |
| 1971 | 0.415 | 0.104 | 0.311 | 0.113 |
| 1972 | 0.419 | 0.107 | 0.316 | 0.116 |
| 1973 | 0.417 | 0.104 | 0.314 | 0.114 |
| 1974 | 0.415 | 0.104 | 0.313 | 0.113 |
| 1975 | 0.419 | 0.106 | 0.315 | 0.115 |
| 1976 | 0.419 | 0.106 | 0.315 | 0.115 |
| 1977 | 0.426 | 0.109 | 0.321 | 0.120 |
| 1978 | 0.427 | 0.108 | 0.321 | 0.120 |
| 1979 | 0.427 | 0.111 | 0.322 | 0.120 |
| 1980 | 0.428 | 0.112 | 0.323 | 0.121 |
| 1981 | 0.435 | 0.114 | 0.329 | 0.124 |
| 1982 | 0.447 | 0.118 | 0.338 | 0.132 |
| 1983 | 0.447 | 0.120 | 0.339 | 0.132 |
| 1984 | 0.449 | 0.121 | 0.341 | 0.133 |

income inequality in this particular data set, has been very stable over the 40 year period under consideration. We now examine possible macro-effects that may be in part responsible for these observed graduations below, beginning in Chapter IV.

*Notes*

1. See Theil (1967) for a complete exposition.
2. See Slottje (1987) for further discussion.

# Chapter IV

# *Relative Price Changes and Inequality* *

## I. INTRODUCTION

In recent years the analysis of income inequality has undergone a rigorous transformation. As we noted in Chapter III, for many years economists were primarily concerned with questions pertaining to the generation and measurement of the size distribution of total income.[1] Beginning with the seminal work of Theil (1967), Atkinson (1970) and Sen (1970, 1973, 1974), however, a new systematic approach to studying income inequality has been evolving. The new approach has focused on three major issues. The first issue concerns analysis of the properties of various measures of income inequality with the emphasis on additive decomposition characteristics of these measures (cf. Theil, 1967; Atkinson, 1970; Cowell, 1980; Shorrocks, 1980, 1982; and King, 1983).[2] The second issue concerns the decomposition of income inequality by income components: Fei et al. (1978), Theil (1979) and Shorrocks (1982, 1983) have all addressed this question. Finally, some have questioned whether so much emphasis should be placed on income inequality, per se, since income is only one aspect of welfare. Franklin Fisher (1956) long ago made this point, but only recently did researchers begin to utilize other available information in making welfare valuations. Kolm (1977) and Atkinson and Bour-

*This chapter is based primarily on Slottje (1987).

**43**

guignon (1982) referred to this departure from the traditional view as a "multidimensional" approach to analyzing economic inequality. The emphasis in both papers is on the theoretical properties of multidimensional distributions. Maasoumi (1986) and Jorgenson and Slesnick (1984) attempted to actually measure multidimensional economic inequality by incorporating information about schooling, quality of life indices, and distributions of expenditures into their analysis. Maasoumi (1986) based his analysis on information criterion developed by Theil (1967) where a measure of overall (multivariate) inequality is proposed that first constructs aggregate share vectors of various attributes and then proceeds to measure inequality in the representative distributions so obtained. As Maasoumi (1986) notes, another approach to analyzing overall economic inequality would be a method that relies on specified multivariate factor distributions. Maasoumi elaborates that the second approach would involve the use of joint and single factor marginal distributions, which would yield measures of concentration and variation that are simple to evaluate.

The purpose of this chapter is to introduce the comprehensive model of economic inequality that we will utilize throughout the rest of the book. We begin by examining the impact of relative price changes on inequality in the marginal distributions of various income components where the marginal distributions are derived from a multidimensional joint distribution. The model would also be useful in analyzing marginal expenditure distributions, unfortunately the data do not exist to explore these marginal distributions at this time. As Parks (1978) notes, changes in relative prices occur in response to changes in many determinants of supply and demand. Parks lays out a rigorous definition for the concept of a relative price that is utilized below. A number of studies have analyzed the impact of inflation (as measured by some broad based index) on the size distribution of total income.[3] This chapter provides a synthesis of much of the work previously discussed. The analysis uses a multidimensional joint distribution function of components of income and expenditures on various commodity groups, and derive Gini measures of inequality from marginal distributions of the various income components. The Gini measures are shown to depend on the parameters of the multidimensional joint distribution function. It is then demonstrated that the parameters of the multidimensional joint distribution depend on the relative prices of various commodity groups, and several other specified exogenous economic variables. Thus, knowledge of how changes in relative prices (and other specified variables) affect the parameters of the multidimensional joint distribution is deductively equivalent to knowledge of how changes in relative prices, (and other specified variables) affect inequality in the marginal distributions of various components of income. Section II contains the model and section three the empirical results, conclusions are summarized in Section IV.

## II. THE MODEL

In order to analyze the impact of relative price changes on inequality in the marginal distribution of various income components, which are derived from a multidimensional joint distribution function, a technique is developed that allows for description and manipulation of entire joint distributions. With a view to the feasibility of actual application the beta distribution of the second kind will be used in this study.[4] The model of inequality is composed of two main parts. The cross-section model is a specified multivariate distribution of receipts of income from various sources and expenditures on various commodity groups. Inequalities in the marginal distributions of the various components of income depend on the parameters of the joint distribution. The parameters are allowed to change from year to year. The intertemporal model (of the parameters of the cross-section model) relates year-to-year changes in the joint distribution to changes in specified exogenous variables. As is demonstrated below, the intertemporal model predicts year-to-year changes in various measures of inequality in the various marginal income distributions under the impact of such exogenous variables.

Let the cross-section model of the joint density of expenditures on commodities and components of income be defined as follows:

$$g(m_1, \ldots, m_n, w_l; a_1, \ldots, a_n, c_1, \ldots, c_l, K, b^*)$$

$$= \frac{K^{b^*} \, m_1^{a_1-1} \ldots m_n^{a_n-1} \, w_1^{c_1-1} \ldots w_l^{c_l-1}}{B(a_1, \ldots, a_n, c_1, \ldots, c_l, b^*) \, [K + m \, w]^{b^*+c+a}} \quad (4.1)$$

$$m_i > 0, \; w_j > 0 \qquad c = c_1 + \ldots \ldots + c_l$$

$$= 0 \text{ otherwise see Eq. (4.4)}$$

where expenditure on commodity group $i$ is $m_i$, $i = 1, \ldots, n$. Total expenditure on all commodities is $m$,

$$m = m_1 + \ldots + m_n. \tag{4.2}$$

Define $w_j$ as income from source $j$, $j = 1, \ldots, P$. Total income $w$ is defined as

$$w = w_1 + \ldots + w_l. \tag{4.3}$$

The beta B( ) is defined in Kendall and Stuart (1958, pp. 150–151). The $K$ in Eq. (4.1) is called the Pareto lower terminal and $b^*$ the generalized Pareto parameter because under certain restrictions on the $a_i$'s, $b^*$ and $c_j$'s, Eq. (4.1) becomes the familiar Pareto distribution.[5] The $a_i$'s and $c_j$'s are called intercommodity and interincome inequality parameters respectively. Using Eq. (4.1) the marginal distributions of income for various components are derived by standard integration. Thus for the $j$th income component we have the marginal density given as

$$g(w_j) = \frac{K^{b^*} \, w_j^{c_j-1}}{B(c_j, \, b^*) \, [K + w_j]^{b^*+c}}$$

$$w_j > 0, \, c_j > 0, j = 1, \ldots \ldots, l \tag{4.4}$$

$$= 0 \text{ otherwise.}$$

It is, of course, possible to find many measures of inequality in the marginal density of income component $j$. The Gini coefficient will be used since it satisfies Champernowne's (1974) criteria of what a statistic of inequality should actually measure. The Gini coefficient derived from Eq. (4.4) is

$$G_{w_j}(c_j, b^*) = \frac{\Gamma(c_j + b^*)\Gamma(c_j + 1/2)\Gamma(b^* + 1/2)}{\Gamma(1/2)\Gamma)c_j + 1)\Gamma(c_j + b^* + 1/2)\Gamma(b^*)} \cdot \left[1 + \frac{2c_j}{2b^* - 1}\right] \tag{4.5}$$

The gamma distribution, $Q( )$, is defined in Kendall and Stuart (1958, pp. 152–153). This demonstrates that inequality in the marginal distribution of the $j$th income component (as measured by the Gini coefficient) depends on the values of the $b^*$ and $c_j$. The $b^*$, $c_j$'s and $c$ are found by the generalized variance method of moments (see Elderton [1938]), by relating the means and variances of actual empirical data to the parameters of the hypothetical distribution (cf. Slottje, 1984). The behavior of the $c_j$'s and $b^*$ in Eq. (4.5) is such that if both $c_j$ and $b^*$ increase together or one increases and the other is constant then the Gini coefficient falls. This means that if $c_j$ and $b*$ increase together or one increases (and the other is constant) that the amount of inequality in the marginal distribution of the $j$th income component decreases. A very attractive feature of the beta distribution of the second kind concerns the fact that by summing the $w_j$'s we can derive the marginal distribution of total income, $w$, which has exactly the same form as Eq. (4.4) except the $c_j$'s are replaced by $c$. The inequality measure Eq. (4.5) is also the same for total income except that $c$ replaces $c_j$. The flexibility of this functional form allows us to examine the relationship between total income inequality and inequality in various income components that comprise total income. As Shorrocks (1980, 1982) has noted, this is an attractive property for a statistical distribution used in inequality analysis to exhibit.

The above discussion should make it clear that the effect of exogenous variables on the $b*$, $c_j$'s and $c$ systematically specifies the effect of such variables on inequality in the marginal distribution of various components of income and the marginal distribution of total income. In other words, it is conjectured that the interincome inequality parameters and $b*$ depend on specified exogenous variables in the following way:

$$b* \text{ or } c_j \text{ or } c = \theta \prod_{i=1}^{6} RP^{\gamma i} \prod_{k=1}^{4} Z_k^{ak} e^u \qquad (4.6)$$

$j = 1, \ldots, 10$ (time scripts omitted for ease of exposition)

The $b*$ and interincome inequality parameters are conjectured to depend on the relative prices of several commodity groups, $RP_i$, and on several other macroeconomic variables, $Z_k$. The relation conjectured in Eq. (4.6) is utilized because of the straightforward econometric interpretation that can be given to it (as will be explained below). It is, however, just one member of a family of models that might define the relation given in Eq. (4.6). For completeness, a Box-Cox transformation was performed to check for the appropriateness of this functional form (cf. Fomby et al 1984). The tests yielded results consistent with relation in Eq. (4.6).[6] Following Parks (1978) we define the relative price of the $i$th commodity group as $\dfrac{p_{it}}{p_t}$ where $p_t$ is the aggregate price index for the set of commodity groups and $p_{it}$ is the price of the $i$th commodity group in time period $t$. The $p_{it}$'s are themselves indices that were constructed by the Department of Commerce.[7] Six commodity groups are examined, these include: food, alcohol and tobacco ($RP_1$), housing and utilities ($RP_2$), durables ($RP_3$), clothing and nondurable housewares ($RP_4$), medical care and hygienic services ($RP_5$) and transportation and miscellaneous services ($RP_6$). The macroeconomic variables examined include the overall unemployment rate $Z_1$, a standard growth variable (per capita GNP) $Z_2$; a factor share variable (personal income divided by GNP) $Z_3$; and a transfer payment variable (per capita transfer) $Z_4$. The data for these variables are from the *Economic Report of the President, 1983*. These variables are included since they are major macroeconomic factors impacting income inequality.[8] $\theta$ is the intercept and u is the unobserved stochastic disturbance. To analyze the relationship in Eq. (4.6) take the logarithmic derivations or mathematical elasticities. These equations take the form:

$$ln\ c\ or\ ln\ b^*\ or\ ln\ c_j = A + \sum_{i=1}^{6} \gamma_i\ ln\ RP_i + \sum_{k=1}^{4} \alpha_k\ ln\ Z_k + U$$

$$\text{where } U_t = \rho U_{t-1} + \epsilon_t \qquad -1 < \rho < 1 \qquad (4.7)$$

$$\epsilon_t - iid\ N(o,\ \sigma^2 I).$$

and $A = ln\ \theta$.

A first-order autoregressive error is observed in Eq. (4.7),[9] so that the Gauss-Aitken estimation is performed. It should also be noted that tests for heteroskedasticity were done using White's (1980) general test for heteroskedasticity. Heteroskedasticity was not indicated by the data.[10] Multicollinearity was also a concern so the diagnostic tests of Belsey et al. (1980) were employed. Collinearity was not found to be a problem. The Fisherian (1922) reference class for all tests of significance used in this paper is the hypothetical infinite population of random samples of the commodity group relative prices ($RP_i$'s) and the macroeconomic variables ($Z_k$'s) being fixed and identical with those actually used in estimation. Hence, the random disturbance terms are distributed independently of logarithms of the economic variables. Under these circumstances, Gauss-Aitken estimates of the intercept and elasticity terms are unbiased, minimum variance and minimum generalized variance. Also the *F* ratio's for testing null hypotheses are distributed exactly as Snedecor's *F* statistics with determinate degrees of freedom. The results are now reported.

## III. THE EMPIRICAL RESULTS

Use of the model described in Section II requires cross-section data on consumer expenditures as well as data on various income components in frequency form. The expenditure data are from the *Consumer Expenditure Survey, 1972–1973*. The empirical data in frequency form for total income and various components of income are from the *Internal Revenue Service: Statistics of Income*. The $b^*$, $c$ and $c_j$'s are calculated from the empirical data for the years 1952–1981 inclusive. Over the 30 year span the Internal Revenue Service changed income categories, but it was possible to find 10 classifications that were consistent over time; these are given below in Table IV.1. Using the I.R.S. data one can estimate $b^*$ and the interincome inequality parameters for the marginal distributions of ten components of income and for total income. These are given in Table IV.2. Having estimated the $b^*$, $c$ and $c_j$'s, it is possible to

*Table IV.1.* The Components of Income Used in Deriving the Interincome Inequality Parameters

The individual components of income used to derive the interincome inequality parameters were categorized in the following way:

1. Wages and Salaries
2. Income from Dividends
3. Income from Interest on Assets
4. Income from Pensions and Annuities
5. Income from Rents and Royalties
6. Income from Business, Professions and Farms
7. Income from Partnerships
8. Income from Sale of Capital Assets
9. Income from Estates and Trusts
10. Other Income*

Note: The category Other Income includes categories such as Alimony, State Income Tax Refunds, Small Business Corporation Profits and miscellaneous income sources.

*Table IV.2.* The Inequality Parameters Over Time

| Year | C | C1 | C2 | C3 | C4 | C5 | C6 | C7 | C8 | C9 | C10 | b* |
|---|---|---|---|---|---|---|---|---|---|---|---|---|
| 1952 | 14.1487 | 11.4257 | 0.385302 | 0.12226 | 0.037048 | 0.203765 | 1.07069 | 0.577953 | 0.163012 | 0.111145 | 0.051868 | 5.03096 |
| 1953 | 15.1052 | 12.4036 | 0.385941 | 0.13374 | 0.045854 | 0.206345 | 1.10050 | 0.546431 | 0.137563 | 0.110815 | 0.034391 | 5.18895 |
| 1954 | 14.7824 | 11.9876 | 0.453606 | 0.15364 | 0.051214 | 0.201196 | 1.09012 | 0.548717 | 0.215829 | 0.043897 | 0.036581 | 5.03022 |
| 1955 | 17.9369 | 14.4993 | 0.568022 | 0.18513 | 0.046283 | 0.223001 | 1.32959 | 0.652173 | 0.345021 | 0.037868 | 0.050491 | 5.61827 |
| 1956 | 16.4917 | 13.3207 | 0.530340 | 0.17922 | 0.040233 | 0.171903 | 1.31671 | 0.548628 | 0.281629 | 0.036575 | 0.065835 | 5.07462 |
| 1957 | 17.0305 | 13.8778 | 0.557007 | 0.20023 | 0.047327 | 0.196591 | 1.23779 | 0.567928 | 0.211153 | 0.036406 | 0.098295 | 5.20023 |
| 1958 | 14.3850 | 11.6551 | 0.447922 | 0.18764 | 0.045398 | 0.172511 | 1.05928 | 0.472134 | 0.220935 | 0.030265 | 0.093822 | 4.58701 |
| 1959 | 14.9181 | 12.1235 | 0.457882 | 0.21565 | 0.044311 | 0.159520 | 1.05165 | 0.460836 | 0.307224 | 0.295410 | 0.067944 | 4.52947 |
| 1960 | 15.3170 | 12.5592 | 0.463613 | 0.24667 | 0.014859 | 0.163453 | 1.02530 | 0.436866 | 0.258553 | 0.029719 | 0.118875 | 4.60768 |
| 1961 | 15.3430 | 12.4768 | 0.462849 | 0.26448 | 0.017249 | 0.163866 | 1.05794 | 0.419726 | 0.356480 | 0.028748 | 0.094870 | 4.52530 |
| 1962 | 15.7050 | 12.7968 | 0.481402 | 0.32282 | 0.062299 | 0.152916 | 1.08174 | 0.421935 | 0.260523 | 0.031150 | 0.093449 | 4.51126 |
| 1963 | 15.6712 | 12.6965 | 0.485405 | 0.39049 | 0.113894 | 0.138300 | 1.04674 | 0.395917 | 0.276600 | 0.029829 | 0.097623 | 4.40326 |
| 1964 | 15.8805 | 12.8463 | 0.472806 | 0.40266 | 0.124696 | 0.127294 | 1.01835 | 0.387077 | 0.319534 | 0.031174 | 0.150674 | 4.30294 |
| 1965 | 16.0658 | 12.9094 | 0.482500 | 0.41967 | 0.133190 | 0.113086 | 1.04039 | 0.394544 | 0.371927 | 0.032669 | 0.168372 | 4.25014 |
| 1966 | 14.6119 | 11.7916 | 0.434232 | 0.41035 | 0.136783 | 0.102045 | 0.93577 | 0.332188 | 0.314818 | 0.030396 | 0.123756 | 3.88823 |
| 1967 | 14.5859 | 11.7890 | 0.414512 | 0.42682 | 0.143643 | 0.090290 | 0.88032 | 0.330378 | 0.400148 | 0.028729 | 0.082082 | 3.80842 |
| 1968 | 14.7424 | 11.8936 | 0.400080 | 0.44281 | 0.157313 | 0.091280 | 0.84289 | 0.353469 | 0.483592 | 0.029132 | 0.048553 | 3.76964 |
| 1969 | 15.4126 | 12.7398 | 0.402841 | 0.50161 | 0.176243 | 0.085216 | 0.86766 | 0.302131 | 0.381537 | 0.036798 | 0.081343 | 3.91037 |
| 1970 | 15.5680 | 12.8748 | 0.382953 | 0.53218 | 0.190577 | 0.079108 | 0.80726 | 0.332611 | 0.226535 | 0.035958 | 0.106076 | 3.86168 |
| 1971 | 15.9961 | 13.2415 | 0.367043 | 0.58028 | 0.218478 | 0.082148 | 0.80225 | 0.253434 | 0.307617 | 0.036704 | 0.106617 | 3.90158 |
| 1972 | 16.6187 | 13.6788 | 0.368131 | 0.60162 | 0.242012 | 0.086920 | 0.84704 | 0.289733 | 0.374949 | 0.040903 | 0.088624 | 3.92264 |
| 1973 | 16.8459 | 13.8195 | 0.376482 | 0.64748 | 0.266134 | 0.097366 | 0.91199 | 0.223942 | 0.335912 | 0.040569 | 0.126576 | 3.95603 |
| 1974 | 16.5160 | 13.4015 | 0.353864 | 0.67093 | 0.283091 | 0.090589 | 0.70773 | 0.186840 | 0.229304 | 0.050956 | 0.099082 | 4.00111 |
| 1975 | 16.1880 | 13.3560 | 0.367280 | 0.72904 | 0.350711 | 0.088368 | 0.72075 | 0.180879 | 0.236109 | 0.042803 | 0.115983 | 4.04619 |
| 1976 | 16.8896 | 13.9054 | 0.386224 | 0.76577 | 0.387561 | 0.092213 | 0.75641 | 0.184425 | 0.292675 | 0.045438 | 0.073503 | 4.11846 |
| 1977 | 15.4442 | 12.6497 | 0.388875 | 0.71218 | 0.422789 | 0.067827 | 0.65114 | 0.174089 | 0.271308 | 0.036174 | 0.070080 | 3.80804 |
| 1978 | 19.6183 | 16.0696 | 0.467071 | 0.90239 | 0.523966 | 0.084681 | 0.84152 | 0.222289 | 0.371804 | 0.044987 | 0.089974 | 4.53840 |
| 1979 | 15.8936 | 12.8703 | 0.392099 | 0.77255 | 0.428978 | 0.032998 | 0.61629 | 0.294074 | 0.297956 | 0.039792 | 0.148493 | 3.88768 |
| 1980 | 16.9950 | 14.2161 | 0.408430 | 1.07399 | 0.456890 | 0.043513 | 0.56172 | 0.100870 | 0.294710 | 0.048458 | 0.296680 | 4.05583 |
| 1981 | 15.8291 | 13.2708 | 0.334700 | 1.25480 | 0.526000 | 0.027260 | 0.46683 | 0.276810 | 0.275100 | 0.040890 | 0.005960 | 4.17592 |

calculate the estimated Gini measures of inequality for the marginal distributions of the ten components of income and total income using Eq. (4.5). These are reported in Table IV.3. These results are meaningful only if the beta distribution of the second kind is a good approximation to actual empirical data and if the inclusion of the expenditure information improves efficiency of the fit. In fact, by incorporating the expenditure information into the estimation procedure, the sums of squares of error found by subtracting predicted frequencies from actual observed frequencies, (cf. McDonald, 1984; and Slottje, 1984) decrease an average of 10 percent. Summary statistics of these trends in inequality in the marginal distribution of the various income components (and in total income) are reported in Table IV.4. Table IV.4 also reports the mean Gini measure for each income component over time as well as the variance and the range, it is also indicated if a time trend is present. This becomes important later when assessing the impact of relative price changes on inequality. Table IV.4 shows that inequality in the marginal distributions of wages and salaries, dividend income, rent and royalty income, business, professional and farm income, partnership income, estate and trust income, and pensions and annuities income have all demonstrated decreases in inequality from 1952–1981. The marginal distribution of total income also shows an increasing trend for the years examined.

As is obvious from Table IV.4, there is significant difference in the amount of inequality in the marginal distribution of total income vis à vis most of the income components. Policymakers concerned with distributional effects are ignoring much policy-relevant information when they focus only on total income. It should be noted that meaningful comparisons between the marginal distributions are possible because of the flexibility of the beta distribution of the second kind. As a simple counter-example, assume that the income components were all lognormally distributed. It is well known that the sum of lognormal random variables are not lognormal, thus comparisons of various components vis à vis total income would be very difficult. We also present plots of all the inequality measures and parameters so trends and patterns can be explored by the interested reader. These are given in Figures IV.1–IV.34. We present overlays in Figures IV.24–IV.34 so the reader can see how the inequality parameter movements are related to changes in the Gini coefficients.

## Table IV.3.   The Various Gini Measures Over Time

| Year | G | G1 | G2 | G3 | G4 | G5 | G6 | G7 | G8 | G9 | G0 | b* |
|------|------|------|------|------|------|------|------|------|------|------|------|------|
| 1952 | 0.308228 | 0.315984 | 0.716680 | 0.874105 | 0.956071 | 0.813473 | 0.544197 | 0.647749 | 0.842023 | 0.883559 | 0.940083 | 5.03096 |
| 1953 | 0.301865 | 0.308689 | 0.715359 | 0.864207 | 0.946294 | 0.811112 | 0.537882 | 0.656092 | 0.861128 | 0.883451 | 0.958892 | 5.18895 |
| 1954 | 0.306825 | 0.314139 | 0.689280 | 0.849067 | 0.940772 | 0.815183 | 0.541346 | 0.656695 | 0.805616 | 0.948579 | 0.956589 | 5.03022 |
| 1955. | 0.286143 | 0.292814 | 0.646157 | 0.824076 | 0.945405 | 0.798681 | 0.503388 | 0.621972 | 0.731490 | 0.954663 | 0.940877 | 5.61827 |
| 1956 | 0.302263 | 0.309093 | 0.662182 | 0.830115 | 0.952520 | 0.835354 | 0.511546 | 0.656343 | 0.766544 | 0.956555 | 0.925678 | 5.07462 |
| 1957 | 0.297942 | 0.304369 | 0.652685 | 0.815137 | 0.944699 | 0.817592 | 0.519311 | 0.649324 | 0.807913 | 0.956631 | 0.894526 | 5.20023 |
| 1958 | 0.321043 | 0.328202 | 0.695154 | 0.826364 | 0.947529 | 0.836925 | 0.552080 | 0.686333 | 0.804611 | 0.964061 | 0.900067 | 4.58701 |
| 1959 | 0.321852 | 0.328636 | 0.692030 | 0.808261 | 0.948768 | 0.846613 | 0.554110 | 0.690954 | 0.756594 | 0.762627 | 0.924588 | 4.52947 |
| 1960 | 0.318466 | 0.324847 | 0.689193 | 0.788934 | 0.981838 | 0.843375 | 0.556899 | 0.699135 | 0.782083 | 0.964655 | 0.878235 | 4.60768 |
| 1961 | 0.321165 | 0.327761 | 0.690266 | 0.779280 | 0.979057 | 0.843443 | 0.553243 | 0.706537 | 0.733172 | 0.965826 | 0.899296 | 4.52530 |
| 1962 | 0.320973 | 0.327357 | 0.683822 | 0.749021 | 0.930223 | 0.851617 | 0.550003 | 0.705800 | 0.781593 | 0.963146 | 0.900617 | 4.51126 |
| 1963 | 0.324817 | 0.331319 | 0.683570 | 0.719516 | 0.883128 | 0.863299 | 0.556896 | 0.717270 | 0.773487 | 0.964735 | 0.897205 | 4.40326 |
| 1964 | 0.328128 | 0.334521 | 0.689061 | 0.715498 | 0.874571 | 0.872467 | 0.562897 | 0.721907 | 0.752323 | 0.963348 | 0.854259 | 4.30294 |
| 1965 | 0.329817 | 0.336319 | 0.686296 | 0.709296 | 0.867988 | 0.884382 | 0.560512 | 0.719345 | 0.728856 | 0.961760 | 0.841568 | 4.25014 |
| 1966 | 0.347503 | 0.354057 | 0.708107 | 0.717202 | 0.867007 | 0.895266 | 0.583994 | 0.750412 | 0.758611 | 0.964744 | 0.877250 | 3.88823 |
| 1967 | 0.351236 | 0.357665 | 0.716655 | 0.711972 | 0.862255 | 0.905876 | 0.595190 | 0.752168 | 0.722271 | 0.966689 | 0.913267 | 3.80842 |
| 1968 | 0.352791 | 0.359180 | 0.722825 | 0.706629 | 0.852437 | 0.905163 | 0.602821 | 0.742245 | 0.692415 | 0.966304 | 0.945763 | 3.76964 |
| 1969 | 0.345054 | 0.350569 | 0.719873 | 0.684338 | 0.838135 | 0.910031 | 0.595352 | 0.764581 | 0.728522 | 0.957772 | 0.913568 | 3.91037 |
| 1970 | 0.347007 | 0.352415 | 0.728540 | 0.675396 | 0.828835 | 0.915801 | 0.607748 | 0.750518 | 0.806251 | 0.958757 | 0.891950 | 3.86168 |
| 1971 | 0.344480 | 0.349765 | 0.734741 | 0.660586 | 0.810793 | 0.912860 | 0.607960 | 0.790335 | 0.761967 | 0.957888 | 0.891309 | 3.90158 |
| 1972 | 0.342563 | 0.347857 | 0.734024 | 0.654319 | 0.796632 | 0.908442 | 0.598910 | 0.770709 | 0.731129 | 0.953382 | 0.906908 | 3.92264 |
| 1973 | 0.340735 | 0.346091 | 0.730087 | 0.641719 | 0.782833 | 0.899032 | 0.586612 | 0.807023 | 0.747942 | 0.953674 | 0.874646 | 3.95603 |
| 1974 | 0.339255 | 0.345076 | 0.739341 | 0.635143 | 0.773383 | 0.904851 | 0.626406 | 0.830318 | 0.803435 | 0.942771 | 0.897353 | 4.00111 |
| 1975 | 0.337841 | 0.343290 | 0.732981 | 0.620804 | 0.740257 | 0.906685 | 0.622670 | 0.834051 | 0.799058 | 0.951148 | 0.882818 | 4.04619 |
| 1976 | 0.333742 | 0.339111 | 0.724174 | 0.611585 | 0.723619 | 0.902974 | 0.613589 | 0.831176 | 0.767346 | 0.948247 | 0.920232 | 4.11848 |
| 1977 | 0.349723 | 0.355421 | 0.726805 | 0.628867 | 0.713499 | 0.926594 | 0.643368 | 0.840342 | 0.781487 | 0.958620 | 0.924446 | 3.80804 |
| 1978 | 0.314278 | 0.319399 | 0.688617 | 0.578375 | 0.669273 | 0.908574 | 0.589763 | 0.804045 | 0.726274 | 0.948036 | 0.903697 | 4.53840 |
| 1979 | 0.345278 | 0.351257 | 0.724469 | 0.614263 | 0.710077 | 0.961908 | 0.650947 | 0.768855 | 0.766900 | 0.954621 | 0.858139 | 3.88768 |
| 1980 | 0.336195 | 0.341018 | 0.715886 | 0.559391 | 0.697652 | 0.950383 | 0.663600 | 0.895581 | 0.766880 | 0.945225 | 0.765879 | 4.05583 |
| 1981 | 0.333119 | 0.338273 | 0.746261 | 0.533786 | 0.672865 | 0.967856 | 0.692639 | 0.775155 | 0.776071 | 0.952955 | 0.992687 | 4.17592 |

*Table IV.4.*   Statistics of Gini Measures

| Gini Measures of | Mean | Variance | Minimum Value | Maximum Value | Time Trend |
|---|---|---|---|---|---|
| Total Income | .324 | .00034 | .286 | .352 | Increased |
| Wages and Salaries | .333 | .0033 | .292 | .359 | Increased |
| Dividend Income | .703 | .0067 | .646 | .741 | Increased |
| Interest Income | .728 | .0074 | .578 | .874 | Decreased |
| Pension and Annuities Income | .864 | .0079 | .669 | .981 | Increased |
| Rent and Royalties | .871 | .0015 | .798 | .926 | Increased |
| Business, Profession and Farm Income | .572 | .0013 | .503 | .663 | Increased |
| Partnerships Income | .733 | .0042 | .621 | .895 | Increased |
| Sale of Capital Assets Income | .768 | .0015 | .692 | .861 | Increased |
| Estates and Trust Income | .952 | .00043 | .883 | .966 | Increased |
| Other Income | .905 | .00082 | .841 | .958 | No Trend |

*Note*: The time trend was found by regressing the Gini measures against time with an appropriate adjustment for autocorrelation.

Given these trends in inequality in the marginal distributions of the various income components (and total income) we turn to another question; how have changes in the relative prices of various commodity groups overtime impacted inequality in the marginal distributions of various components of income? As noted, several studies examined the impact of an overall inflation rate on total income inequality. Bach and Ando (1957) did not detect any empirical evidence for the hypothesis that inflation impacts total income inequality and concluded that inflationary redistributional pressures on income are anticipated and effectively taken into account by different economic groups and individuals.[11] As noted earlier, Parks (1978) discussed possible causes of relative price changes. On the supply side, changes in technology, mistakes in suppliers price expectations brought about by unanticipated inflation and resource availability all may cause continuous changes in relative prices. A change in aggregate demand may cause continuous changes in relative prices. A change in aggregate demand may cause different responses (in relative prices) in different markets because of differences in the information con-

(*Text continues on page 88*)

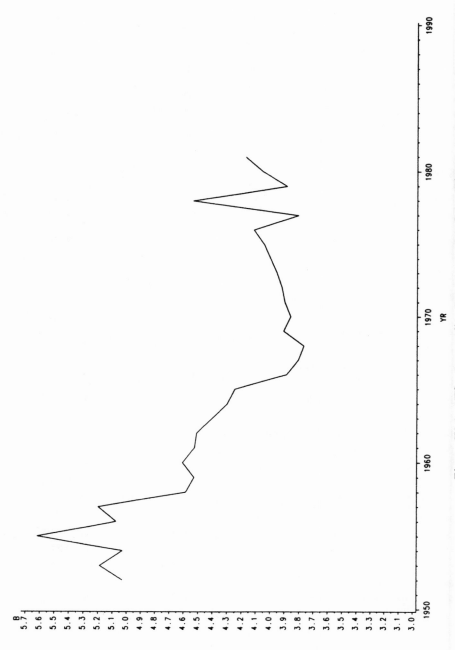

*Figure IV.1.*  The Inequality Parameter B* Over Time

54

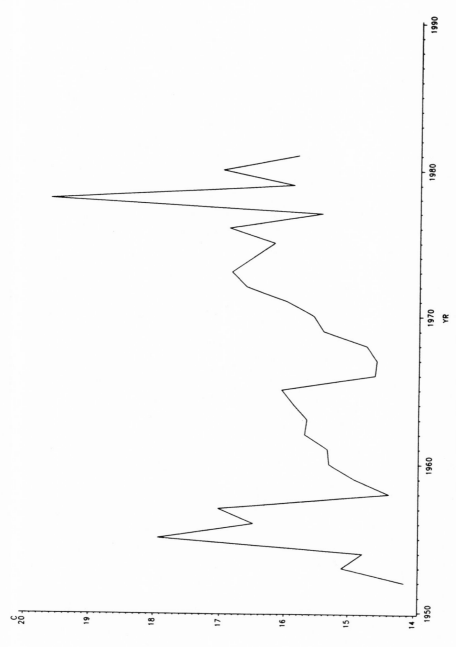

*Figure IV.2.* The Inequality Parameter C Over Time

55

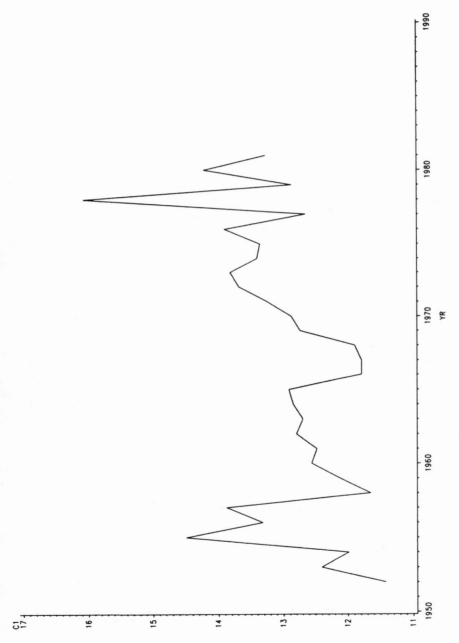

*Figure IV.3.* The Inequality Parameter C1 Over Time

56

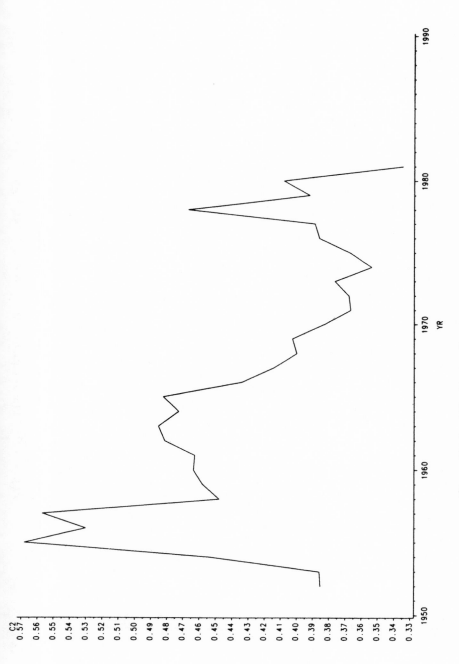

*Figure IV.4.* The Inequality Parameter C2 Over Time

57

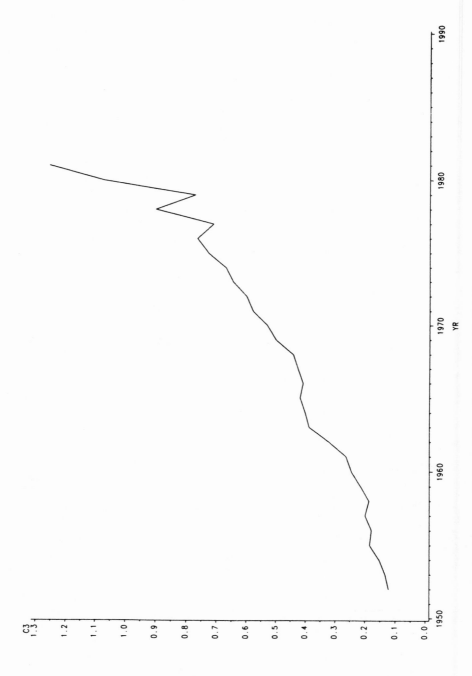

*Figure IV.5.* The Inequality Parameter C3 Over Time

58

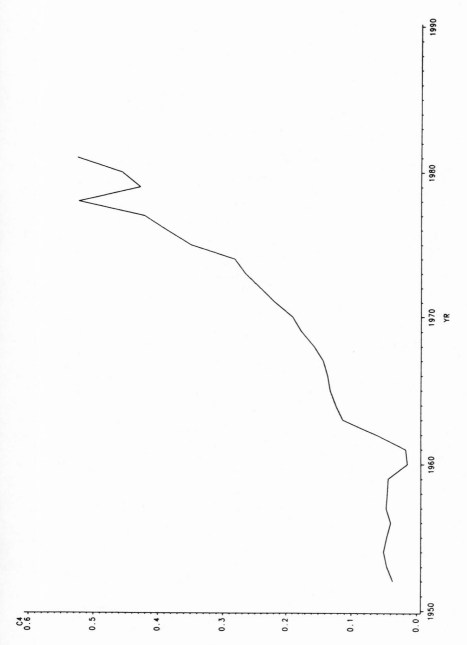

*Figure IV.6.*   The Inequality Parameter C4 Over Time

59

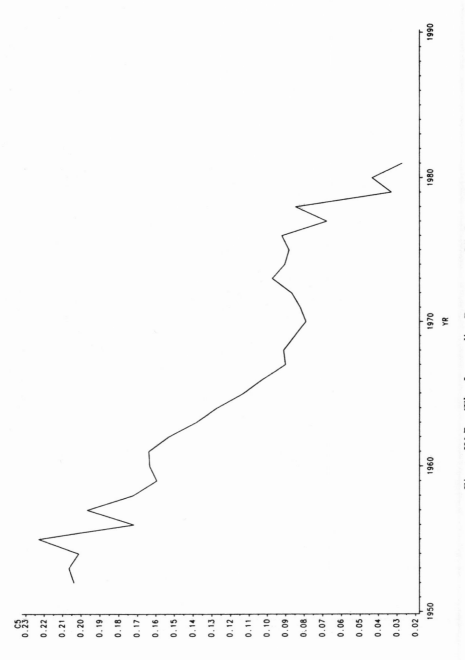

*Figure IV.7.* The Inequality Parameter C5 Over Time

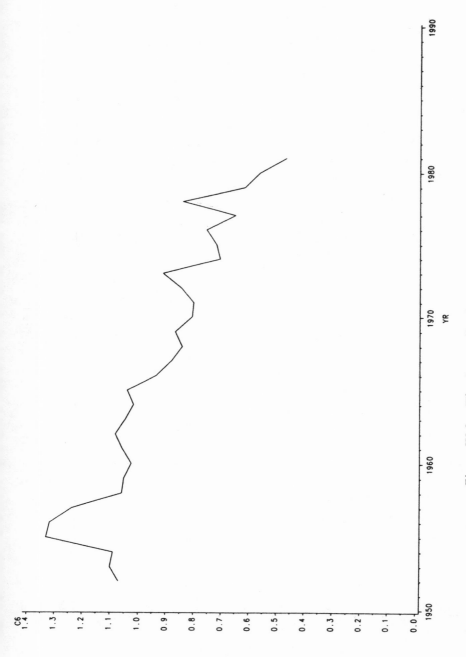

*Figure IV.8.* The Inequality Parameter C6 Over Time

61

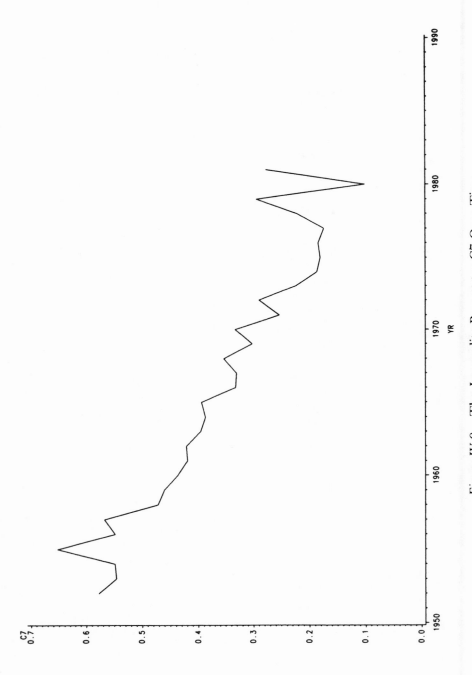

*Figure IV.9.* The Inequality Parameter C7 Over Time

62

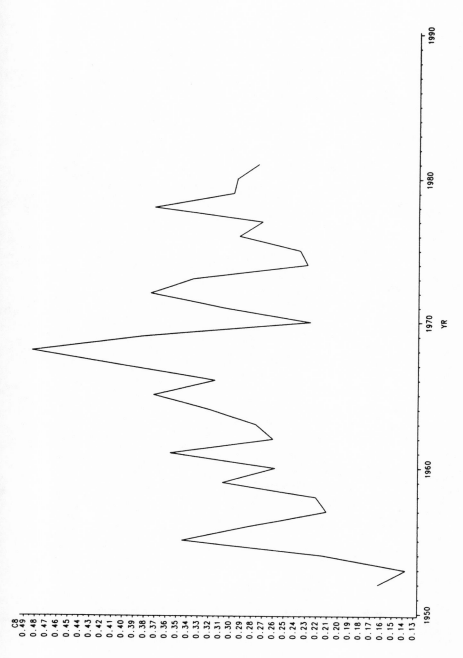

*Figure IV.10.* The Inequality Parameter C8 Over Time

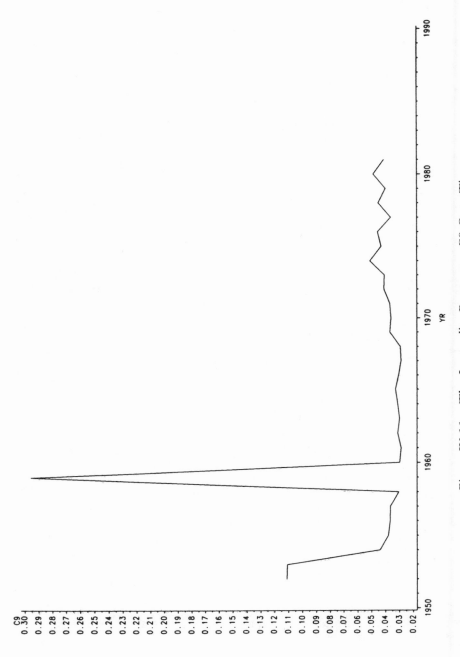

*Figure IV.11.* The Inequality Parameter C9 Over Time

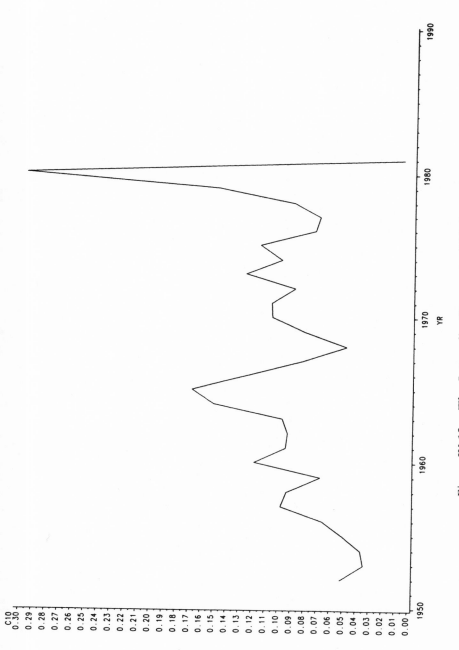

*Figure IV.12.* The Inequality Parameter C10 Over Time

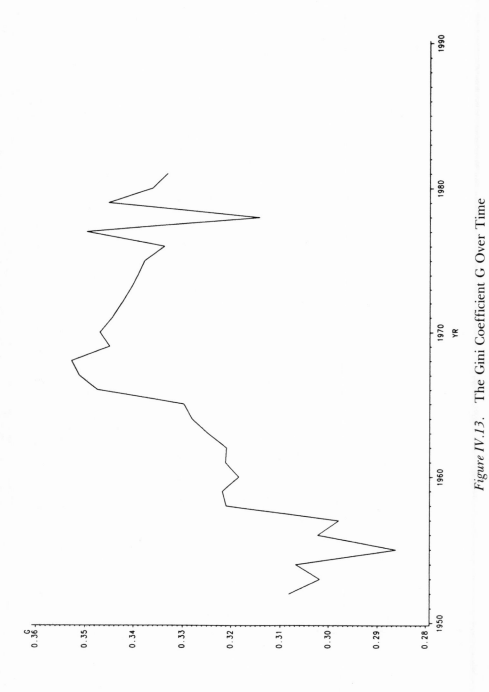

*Figure IV.13.* The Gini Coefficient G Over Time

66

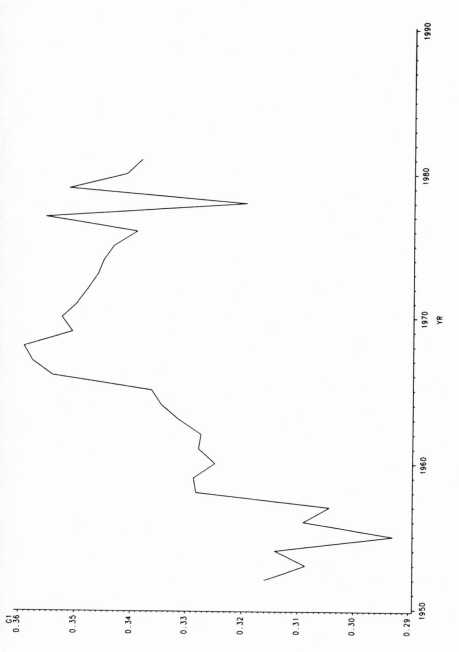

*Figure IV.14.* The Gini Coefficient G1 Over Time

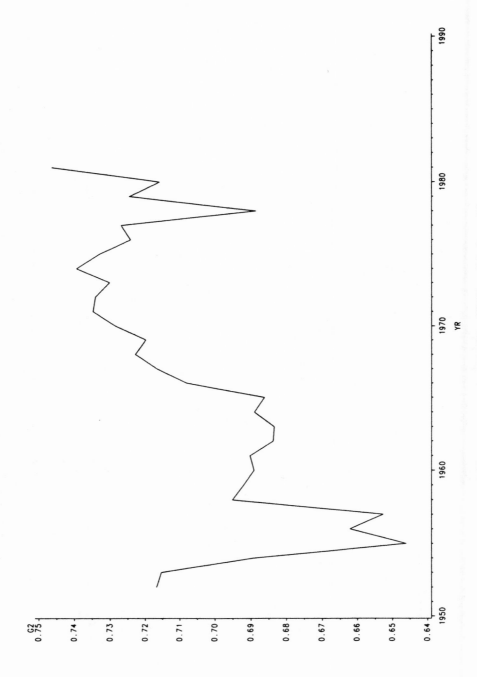

*Figure IV.15.* The Gini Coefficient G2 Over Time

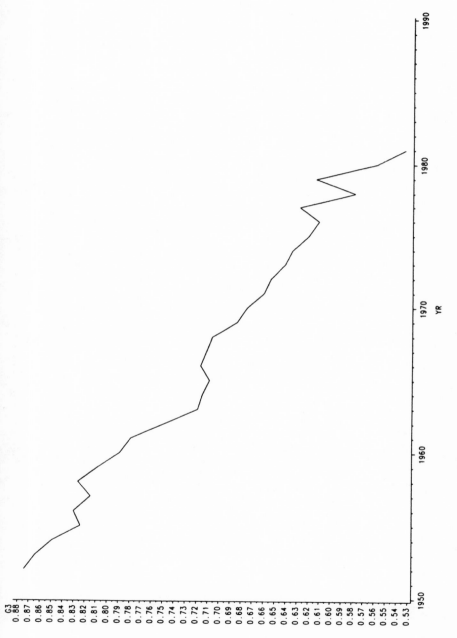

*Figure IV.16.* The Gini Coefficient G3 Over Time

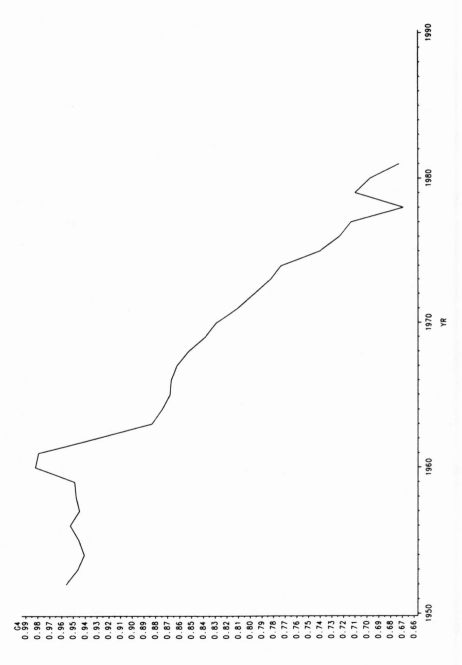

*Figure IV.17.* The Gini Coefficient G4 Over Time

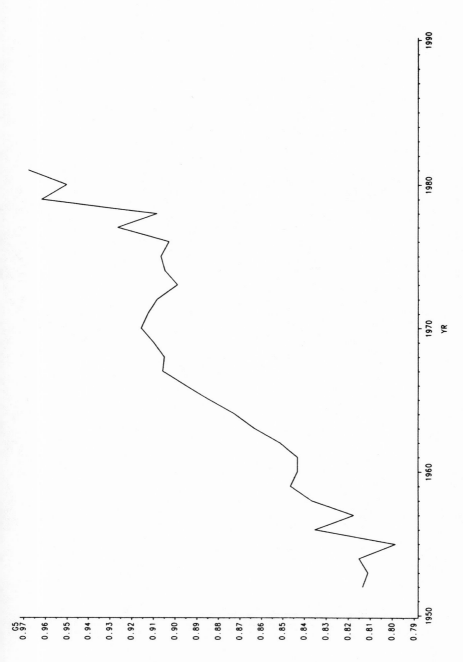

*Figure IV.18.* The Gini Coefficient G5 Over Time

**71**

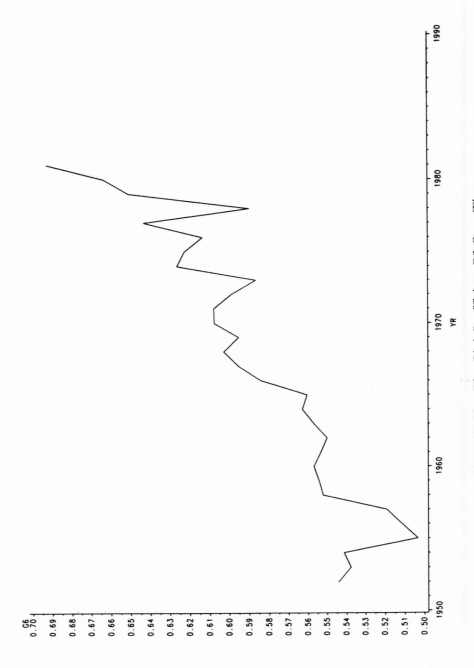

*Figure IV.19.*   The Gini Coefficient G6 Over Time

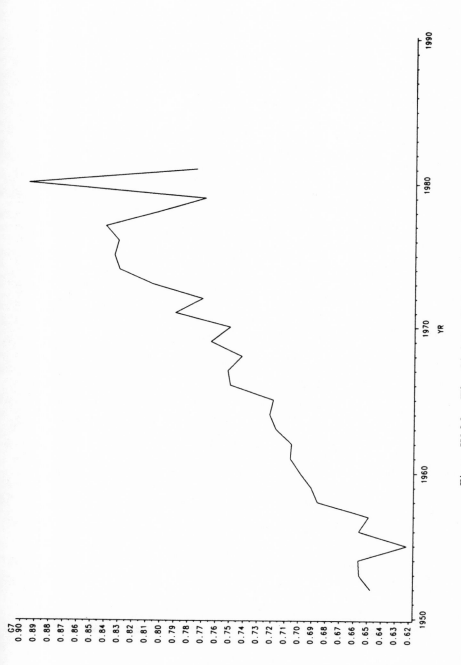

*Figure IV.20.* The Gini Coefficient G7 Over Time

73

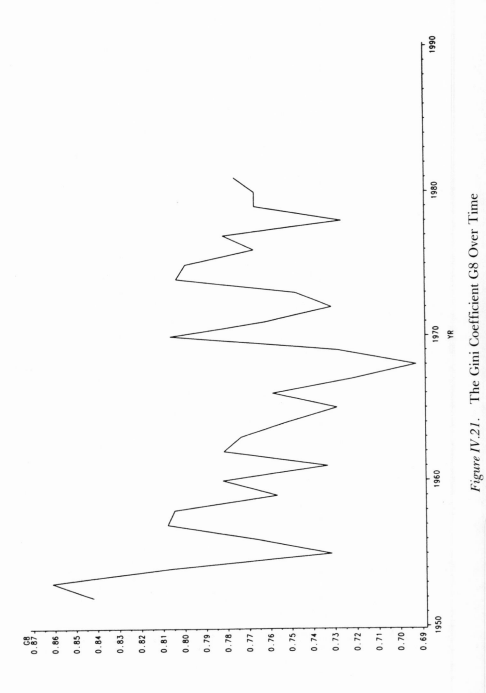

*Figure IV.21.* The Gini Coefficient G8 Over Time

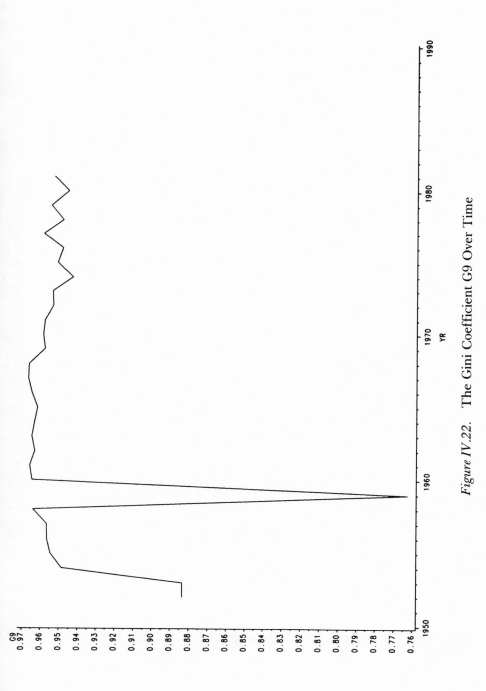

*Figure IV.22.* The Gini Coefficient G9 Over Time

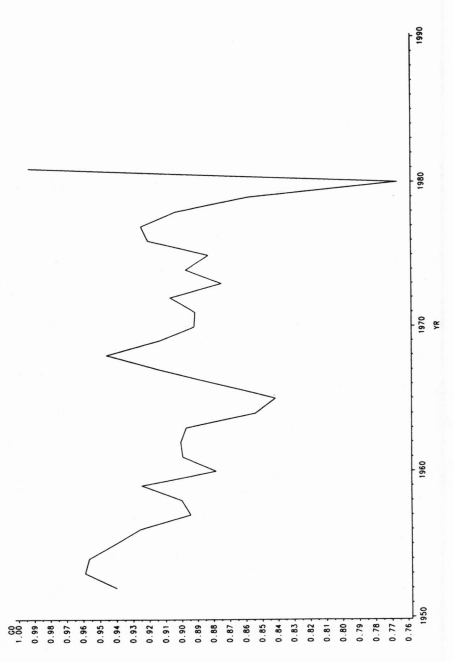

*Figure IV.23.* The Gini Coefficient G10 Over Time

76

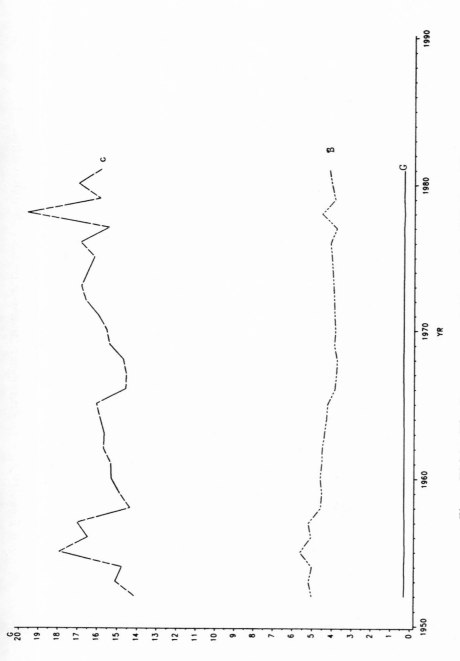

*Figure IV.24.* The Parameters and Measure for C/G Over Time

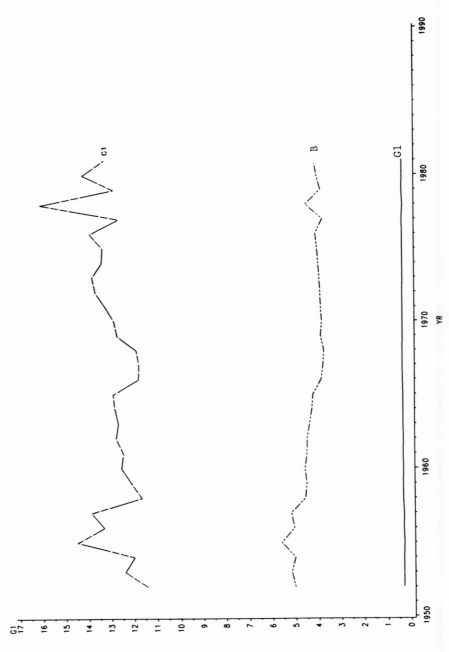

*Figure IV.25.* The Parameters and Measure for C1/G1 Over Time

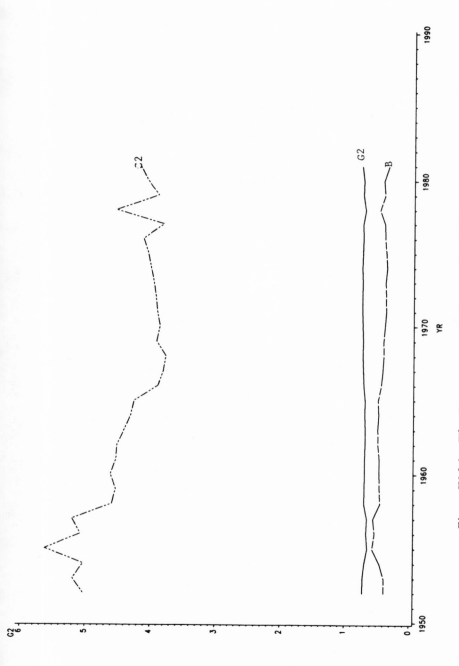

*Figure IV.26.* The Parameters and Measure for C2/G2 Over Time

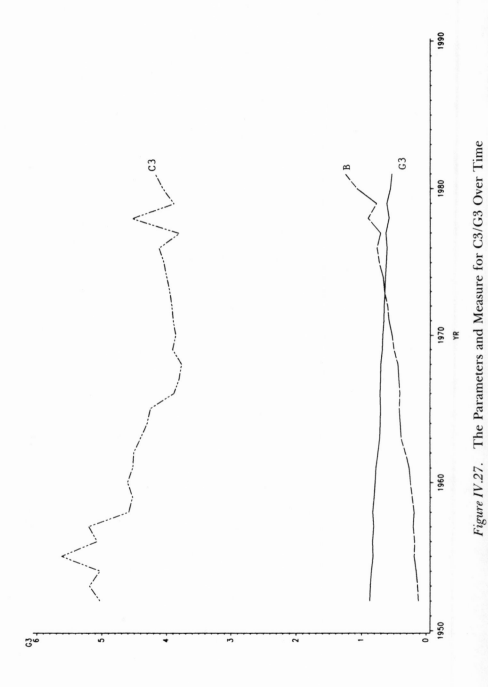

*Figure IV.27.* The Parameters and Measure for C3/G3 Over Time

80

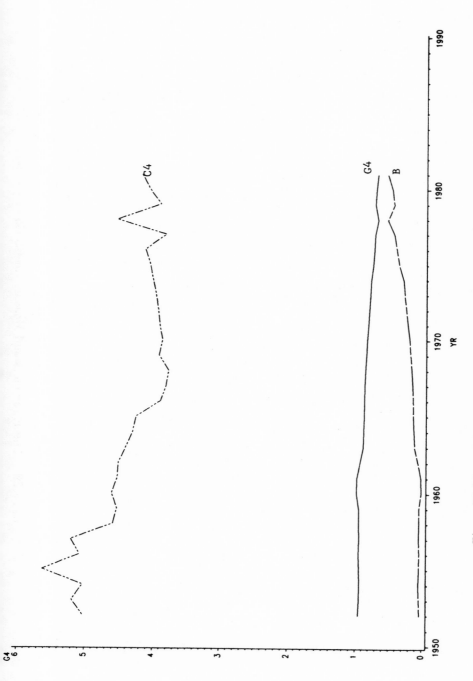

*Figure IV.28.* The Parameters and Measure for C4/G4 Over Time

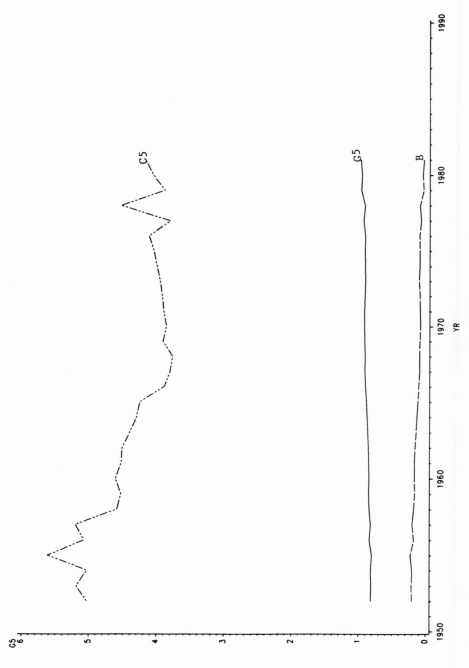

*Figure IV.29.* The Parameters and Measure for C5/G5 Over Time

82

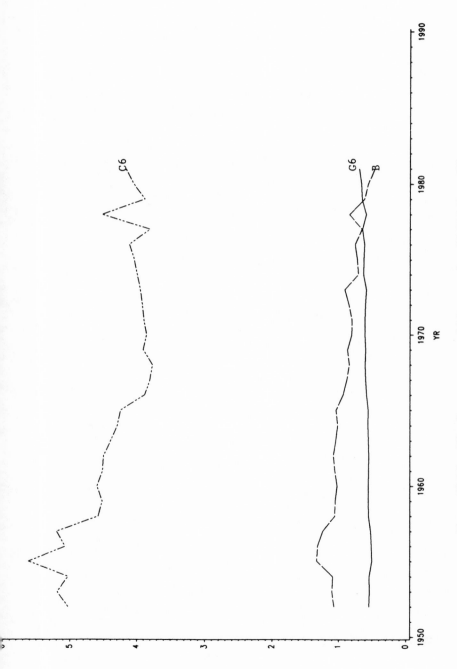

*Figure IV.30.* The Parameters and Measure for C6/G6 Over Time

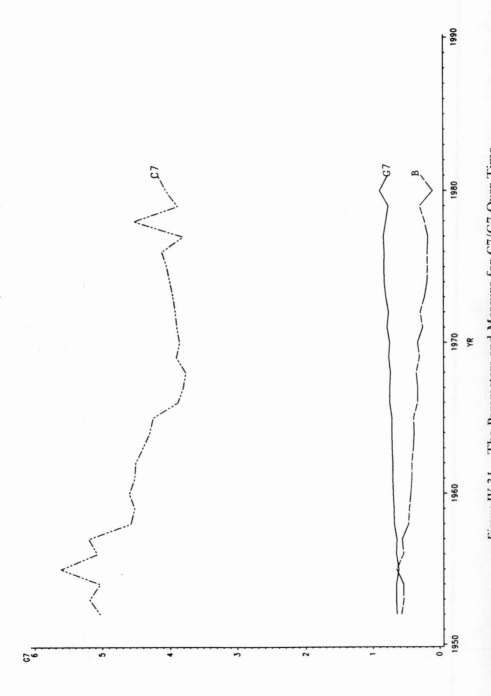

Figure IV.31. The Parameters and Measure for C7/C7 Over Time

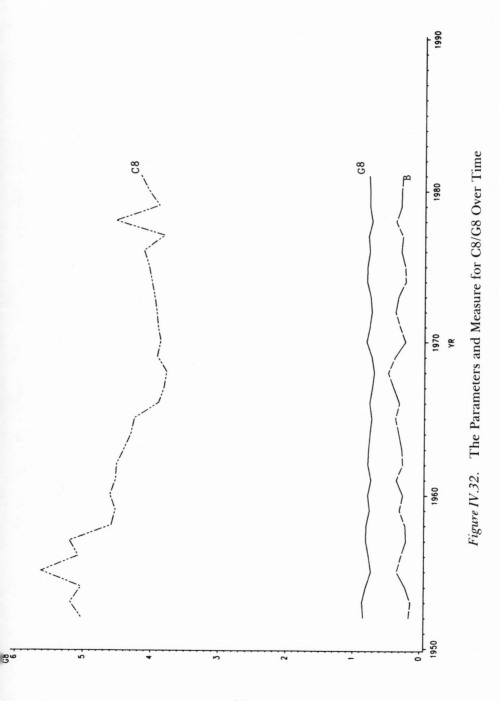

*Figure IV.32.* The Parameters and Measure for C8/G8 Over Time

85

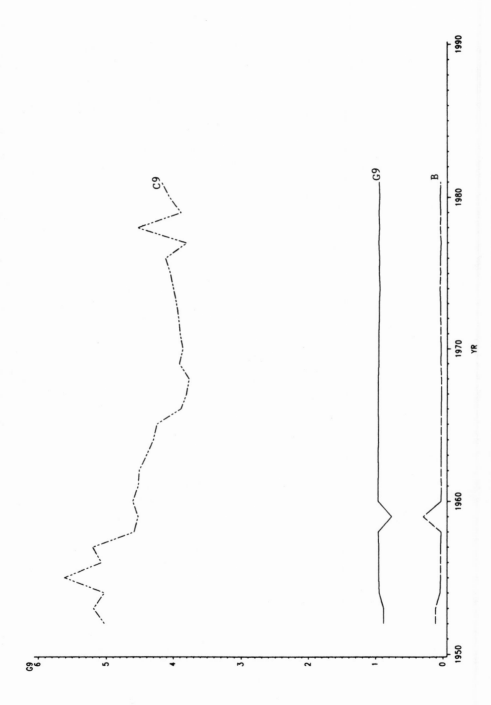

*Figure IV.33.* The Parameters and Measure for C9/G9 Over Time

86

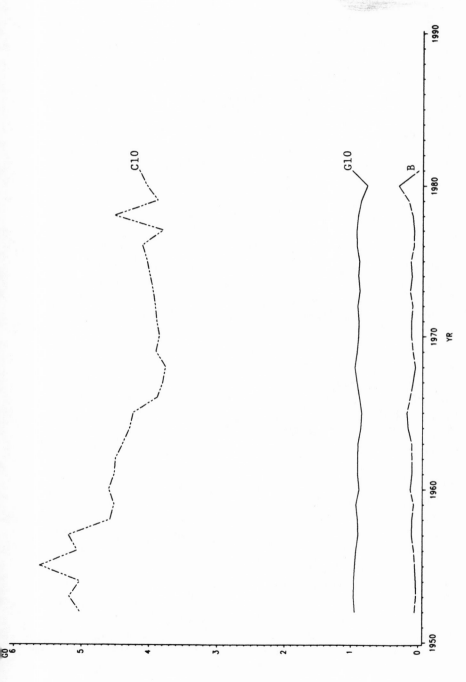

*Figure IV.34.* The Parameters and Measure for C10/G10 Over Time

87

tent of the change.[12] Thus, if we find that relative price changes do impact inequality in the various marginal distributions; these price effects are in part reflecting the supply and demand responses discussed above. However, as Stigler (1954) noted, the best way to resolve such questions is just to "go ahead and look."

In Table IV.5 we present the estimates of the model given in Eq. (4.6). Consider first wages and salaries since this component accounted for roughly 80 percent of total income from 1952–1981. From Table IV.5 note that an increase in the rate of unemployment $(Z_1)$ increases inequality in the marginal distribution of wages and salaries income since the elasticities of cÿll and $b*$ with respect to $Z_1$ are both negative and statistically significant at the .10 level.[13] This is not a surprising result. Increases in transfers $(Z_4)$ increases cÿll and $b*$, which decreases inequality in the marginal distribution of wages and salaries income. We also note that an increasing factor share $(Z_3)$ decreases inequality in the marginal distribution of wages and salaries income. One possible explanation for this phenomenon is that as growth occurs, the low income segment of the population may achieve a larger proportional gain in their relative income position than segments of the population with high income. This is particularly feasible if the growth occurs in low-wages labor markets.

Having discussed the macroeconomic variables, consider now the impact of the relative prices of the various commodity groups. From Table IV.5, it is found that an increase in the relative price of housing and utilities $(RP_2)$ decreases inequality in the marginal distribution of wages and salaries income. One possible explanation for this is that as housing becomes relatively more expensive, those at the upper end of the distribution will not be as concerned about increasing their work effort as those in the middle or lower portion of the distribution. As those in the lower portions change their labor-leisure choice towards more labor, inequality should decrease. Provided, of course, that this effect outweighs the affect of new entrants coming into relatively low-wage markets to help battle the higher relative price. Another possible reason for this phenomenon is a simple supply and demand situation. If the demand for housing increases substantially relative to any supply changes, then the relative price of housing should increase. When the demand for housing rises, individuals may move from lower wage occupations into relatively higher wage housing industry.

**Table IV.5.** Partial Elasticities of Interincome Inequality Parameters and $v^*$ with Respect to the Relative Prices of Various Commodity Groups and Macroeconomic Variables

| Elasticity of: | A | Food $RP_1$ | Housing $RP_2$ | Durables $RP_3$ | Clothing $RP_4$ | Medical Care $RP_5$ | Transportation $RP_6$ | Unemployment $Z_1$ | Per Capita GNP $Z_2$ | Factor Share $Z_3$ | Transfers $Z_4$ | $R^2$ | D.F. |
|---|---|---|---|---|---|---|---|---|---|---|---|---|---|
| $C_1$ | 15.08 (.0001) | −.97 (.4074) | 3.19 (.0072) | −.78 (.2601) | 1.29 (.3293) | −2.32 (.0037) | −2.41 (.0525) | −.21 (.0258) | −.34 (.8123) | .87 (.0007) | .13 (.0214) | .85 | 18 |
| $C_2$ | 11.68 (.0272) | 4.52 (.0321) | 8.92 (.0001) | 2.09 (.0885) | 7.46 (.0028) | 2.09 (.2277) | 3.33 (.1006) | .19 (.1460) | −6.39 (.0139) | .86 (.0291) | .19 (.0179) | .89 | 18 |
| $C_3$ | −6.9 (.3999) | −5.49 (.1201) | −7.19 (.0304) | −4.04 (.0708) | −5.79 (.1494) | 1.56 (.5752) | −2.25 (.4787) | .41 (.0632) | −6.86 (.0685) | −.63 (.3173) | .19 (.1773) | .98 | 18 |
| $C_4$ | 10.19 (.7335) | 18.37 (.1583) | −15.89 (.2032) | −14.63 (.0850) | −10.04 (.0463) | −11.36 (.2638) | −15.32 (.1830) | .64 (.0394) | −16.54 (.1939) | 1.01 (.6649) | .22 (.6509) | .87 | 18 |
| $C_5$ | .41 (.9517) | 8.79 (.0036) | 7.48 (.0061) | 2.91 (.0744) | 8.33 (.0111) | 1.76 (.4575) | 1.56 (.5651) | .39 (.0377) | −3.83 (.2623) | .27 (.5787) | .06 (.6198) | .98 | 18 |
| $C_6$ | 13.53 (.0004) | 1.96 (.1331) | 7.22 (.0001) | .69 (.3533) | 3.11 (.0889) | −1.16 (.3028) | −2.46 (.0662) | .15 (.0790) | −2.05 (.2040) | .95 (.0007) | .16 (.0095) | .98 | 18 |
| $C_7$ | 23.93 (.0251) | −1.12 (.7758) | 10.12 (.0105) | 2.78 (.2380) | −1.06 (.8086) | −4.92 (.1660) | −5.54 (.1748) | −.41 (.1375) | 9.65 (.0619) | 1.97 (.0141) | −0.07 (.6617) | .96 | 18 |
| $C_8$ | −8.89 (.5343) | 1.45 (.8016) | 4.48 (.3970) | −1.05 (.7647) | 5.21 (.4160) | 7.37 (.1130) | 4.92 (.3847) | −.06 (.8512) | −13.19 (.0579) | .43 (.6838) | .01 (.9667) | .74 | 18 |
| $C_9$ | 13.09 (.2527) | −7.91 (.0971) | −9.8 (.0269) | −1.7 (.5376) | −8.6 (.0971) | −13.8 (.0018) | −10.1 (.0315) | −.38 (.1971) | 11.26 (.0396) | 1.4 (.1001) | −.24 (.2257) | .89 | 18 |
| $C_@$ | 14.80 (.0001) | −.54 (.6254) | 3.43 (.0030) | −.70 (.2866) | 1.38 (.2754) | −2.04 (.0483) | −2.25 (.0575) | −.20 (.0141) | −1.00 (.4723) | .83 (.0007) | .14 (.0129) | .85 | 18 |
| $b^*$ | 12.98 (.0001) | .38 (.6619) | 3.99 (.0001) | .36 (.4058) | 1.98 (.0560) | −2.56 (.0036) | −1.00 (.2680) | .12 (.0449) | .66 (.5506) | .85 (.0001) | .07 (.0747) | .97 | 18 |

*Notes:* The numbers in parentheses are $Pr\{t_{18} > t/Ho;\beta_i^* = 0\}$

The $R^2$ is the Buse (1973) adjusted coefficient of determination.

D.F. is the number of degrees of freedom for each equation.

@We do not include "other income" since this is a residual component and our model did a poor job in explaining the variation in $c_{10}$. In fact, none of the exogenous variables were statistically significant at a 10% level.

The net effect is to lower inequality because as individuals move out of the relatively lower wage markets, wages should rise in these markets as well. Increases in the relative prices of medical care and hygienic services ($RP_5$), and an increase in the relative price of transportation and miscellaneous goods ($RP_6$) increases inequality in the marginal distribution of wages and salaries income. When the relative price of medical care increases, the price increase will be felt most severely by the elderly and the poor. If they decrease their consumption of medical services they will be ill more often or sustain current illness longer. This will adversely affect the work effort of the poor and ceteris paribus, inequality should increase. These examples were not intended as definitive explanations of how relative price changes impact inequality in the various income components. Rather they are preferred simply to illustrate the type of issues policymakers might address using this comprehensive model.

After the somewhat detailed description of how specified exogenous variables impact inequality in the marginal distribution of wages and salaries above; a brief synopsis of how changes in the exogenous variables affect inequality in the marginal distributions of the other components of income is now presented. For the other 8 components of income, notice that in 48 percent of the possible cases the relative prices of the various commodity groups do impact inequality in the various marginal distributions. In fact, likelihood ratio tests were performed under the null hypothesis that relative prices do not impact inequality in the marginal distribution of each income component. Only the income component sale of capital assets failed to reject this null hypothesis.[14] The relative price of the housing and utilities commodity group affected inequality in the marginal distribution of 7 of 9 components. One possible explanation of this is that as housing prices increase, individuals must adjust their portfolio mix to increasing expenditures on housing and decreasing expenditures on other income earning assets. A significant impact of changes in other relative prices were not nearly as pervasive across the other income components. The macroeconomic variables had a significant impact on inequality in the various marginal distributions in 47 percent of the possible cases. However, likelihood ratio tests failed to reject the null hypothesis that all the $Z_k$'s together do not belong in the model for 6 of 9 income components. Only for the components wages and salaries, dividend income and business, profession and farm income is this hypothesis rejected. Thus, while these standard macroeconomic variables impact inequality in the marginal distribution of wages and salaries, they do not seem to have much impact on most of the other components of income. This may be due to the fact that individuals' relative positions in the marginal distributions of these other income components are less sensitive to changes in market conditions than individuals' relative positions in the marginal distribution of wage and salary income.

Finally, this section is closed by noting that inequality in the marginal distribution of total income is influenced by the specified exogenous variables in much the same fashion that these exogenous variables impact inequality in the marginal distribution of wages and salaries income. This result is not very surprising since wages and salaries comprise such a large portion of total income. The analysis does suggest, however, that the policymaker concerned with overall income inequality should start paying closer attention to changes in relative prices. It must be emphasized again that inflation (if unanticipated) is just one aspect of a change in a relative price. The policymaker whose stated concern is income inequality should perhaps pay less attention to the absolute inflation rate and more attention to the behavior of markets that determine changes in and levels of relative prices. The price data are given in the appendix to this chapter for the interested reader.

## IV. CONCLUDING REMARKS

This chapter demonstrated that one approach to analyzing comprehensive economic inequality is to utilize a multidimensional joint distribution function of various factors. With a view to feasibility and subsequent application, a beta distribution of the second kind was used. This functional form allowed the flexibility to analyze the relationship between total income inequality and the inequality present in the marginal distributions of various income components that comprise total income. Furthermore, the hypothetical form used did fit actual empirical data well by incorporating additional information into the estimation procedure. It was then shown that Gini measures of inequality for the marginal distributions of the various income components can be expressed in terms of the parameters of the multidimensional joint distribution. Thus, conjecturing that specified exogenous variables affect the parameters of the multidimensional joint distribution in a particular way is deductively equivalent to obtaining information on how the specified exogenous variables affect inequality in the marginal distributions of the various components of income.

The framework was developed to analyze the impact of relative price changes on inequality in the marginal distributions of various components of income. While several researchers have analyzed the impact of an overall inflation rate on income inequality, this is the first study to analyze the impact of changes in relative prices (of various commodity groups) on inequality in the marginal distributions of various components of income. It was found that changes in relative prices had a significant impact on inequality in the marginal distributions of several of the components of income, including wage and salaries income. One important implication of this chapter is that policymakers concerned with the size distribution of income should perhaps pay closer attention to stabilizing relative prices instead of focusing on the narrow inflation aspect of a relative price change. We now explore the larger question of various fiscal and monetary policy impacts on inequality in Chapter V.

## NOTES

1. See Sahota (1978) for a survey of this vast literature.

2. See also the work of Blackorby et al. (1980), Kuga (1979), Kakwani (1980) and Foster (1983) on this topic.

3. Bach and Ando (1957) studied this issue as did Kessel and Alchian (1960), Muellbauer (1974), Thurow (1970), Salam and Mount (1974) and Blinder and Esaki (1978).

4. Basmann was the first to demonstrate the merits of this functional form in empirical work on income inequality with actual applications reported in Basmann et al. (1983, 1984).

5. The lower terminal $K$ is important because it permits incorporation of information about expenditures into the estimation. The $K$ is found by locating the individual in a survey with the lowest aggregate income and expenditure figure, define this as $K$. $K$ is so defined because in a joint distribution of income and expenditures, standard economic theory tells us that the covariance between income and expenditure is not zero. If it were zero, then expenditures consumers make would be

statistically independent from the income they earn, which is clearly not the case.

6. The Box-Cox transformation uses the power transformation,

$$y^{(\lambda_1)} = \frac{y^{\lambda_1} - 1}{\lambda_1} \qquad \lambda_1 \neq 0$$

$$= \ln y \qquad \lambda_1 = 0$$

$$y^{(\lambda_2)} = \frac{x^{\lambda_2} - 2}{\lambda_2} \qquad \lambda_2 \neq 0$$

$$= \ln x \qquad \lambda_2 = 0$$

The model specified in (6) (and (7)) corresponds to $\lambda_1 = \lambda_2 = 0$ and fit better than models specified under $\lambda_1 = 0, \lambda_1 = 1$ (semilog), $\lambda_1 = \lambda_2 = 1$ (linear), $\lambda_1 = 1, \lambda_2 = 01$ (reciprocal) and $\lambda_1 = 0, \lambda_2 \neq -1$ (log reciprocal). The $R^2$ used to make these comparisons is discussed in Gujarati (1978, pages 110–111).

7. These indices were kindly provided to us by Laura Blancifioriti from the U.S. Bureau of Labor Statistics. She provided indices for all commodity groups. We aggregated to six to avoid multicollinearity problems.

8. See Thurow (1970) for this discussion.

9. We then use a standard Kadiyala (1968) transformation to adjust for the autocorrelation where the $\rho$ coefficient is chosen by a sensitivity analysis where the criteria for adjustment of the autocorrelation is based upon a standard Durbin-Waton (1950) "d" statistic. AR(2), AR(3), AR(4) and AR(5) processes were also specified with the autoregressive parameters statistically insignificant at a 10 percent level of significance for all the models.

10. It should be noted that the test is a very general one and as an anonymous referee pointed out, tends to over-reject the null hypothesis in small samples. This is *due to the fact that the test is less powerful than specific heteroskedasticity* tests because little information is utilized. The test is based upon the null hypothesis of homoscedasticity

$$Ho: E(e_i^2) = \sigma^2 \, v_i$$

where the test statistic is a $\chi^2 \, k(k + 1)/2$. The test is essentially comparing the elements of $\hat{v}$ and $\hat{\sigma}^2 \, (x'x)$ with $\hat{v} = \sum_{i=1}^{k} \hat{e}_i^2 x_i x_i'$ with $x_i$ and $\hat{e}_i^2 = (y_i - x_i \hat{o})^2$.
In our model the values of $\hat{\chi}^2$ all ranged from 10–22, thus we fail to reject $Ho$ as expected. Again it is a very general test and the sample is not large making the power small.

11. See Bach and Ando (1957), p. 12).

12. See Parks (1978), p. 80).

13. All variables in this study that are called "statistically significant" refer to a 10 percent level of statistical significance.

14. The likelihood ratio test for the null hypothesis that relative prices do not belong on the model was based on the $Pr[F_{6,19} < F/Ho: RP_i\text{'s} = 0]$. For the $Pr[F_{4,19} < F/Ho: Z_k\text{'s} = 0]$.

# DATA APPENDIX FOR CHAPTER IV

## The Six Commodity Groups

In her study, Blanciforti (1982) constructed eleven commodity group price and expenditure indices, which are presented in Appendix Table IV.1 and defined below. From data from the National Income and Product Accounts (NIPA) for the Bureau of Economic Analysis. The 11 commodity groups included:

1. Food,
2. Alcohol and Tobacco,
3. Clothing,
4. Housing,
5. Utilities,
6. Transportation,
7. Medical Care,
8. Durable Goods,
9. Nondurable Goods,
10. Services, and
11. Miscellaneous Goods.

In this study, we have aggregated 6 commodity groups by combining the 11 groups.

Following is a description of expenditure items included in each aggregate group:

| Mnemonic | Explanation |
| --- | --- |
| (1) Food: | Food purchased for off-premise consumption excluding alcohol, purchased meals and beverages. |
| (2) Alcohol and Tobacco: | Alcoholic beverages plus tobacco products. |
| (3) Clothing: | Shoes and other footwear, shoe cleaning and repairing, clothing and accessories except footwear; cleaning, laundering, dyeing, pressing, alteration, storage, and repair of garments; jewelry and watches, other. |
| (4) Housing: | Owner occupied nonfarm dwellings, tenant occupied nonfarm dwellings. |
| (5) Utilities: | Electricity, gas, fuel oil and coal. |

| Mnemonic | Explanation |
| --- | --- |
| (6) Transportation: | Tires, tubes, accessories and other parts; repair, greasing, washing, parking, storage, and rental; gasoline and oil; bridge, tunnel, ferry, and toll roads; insurance premiums less claims made, purchased local transportation, purchased intercity transportation. |
| (7) Medical Care: | Drug preparation and sundries; physicians, dentists and other professional services; privately controlled hospitals and sanitariums; medical care hospital, income loss and workmen's compensation insurance. |
| (8) Durable Goods: | Furniture including mattresses and bedsprings; kitchen and other household appliances; china, glass and tableware, utensils, and other durable household furnishings; books and maps; wheel goods, durable toys, sports equipment; boats and pleasure aircraft; radio and T.V. receivers; new autos, net purchases of used autos; other motor vehicles. |
| (9) Other Nondurables: | Toilet articles and preparations; semidurable household furnishings; cleaning and polishing preparations, miscellaneous household supplies and paper products; stationery and writing supplies; magazines, newspapers, and sheet music; nondurable toys and sport supplies; flowers, seeds, and potted plants. |
| (10) Other Services: | Personal business expenditures; barbers, beauty shops, and baths; water and other sanitary services; telephone and telegraph; domestic services; other household operations; radio and T.V. repair; admissions to spectator amusements; clubs and fraternal organizations; parimutuel net receipts; other recreation; commercial participants amusements. |
| (11) Other Miscellaneous: | Private education and research; religious and welfare activities; net foreign travel; food furnished employees; food produced and consumed on farms; clothing furnished to military personnel; rental value of farm dwellings; other housing; ophthalmic products and orthopedic appliances. |

*Appendix Table IV.1.* Price Data Used in This Study before Aggregated to Six Groups

| Year | P1 | P2 | P3 | P4 | P5 | P6 | P7 | P8 | P9 | P10 | P11 |
|------|------|------|------|------|------|------|------|------|------|------|------|
| 1947 | 46.4 | 56.0 | 62.5 | 51.3 | 58.7 | 42.9 | 42.7 | 65.4 | 61.8 | 36.1 | 53.2 |
| 1948 | 49.2 | 55.4 | 66.1 | 54.7 | 64.7 | 47.2 | 44.7 | 68.1 | 65.8 | 38.0 | 55.8 |
| 1949 | 47.4 | 55.2 | 63.8 | 57.1 | 65.9 | 40.1 | 44.6 | 68.3 | 63.3 | 39.4 | 53.4 |
| 1950 | 48.5 | 54.9 | 63.4 | 59.1 | 67.0 | 52.5 | 45.1 | 70.3 | 63.7 | 40.0 | 53.9 |
| 1951 | 52.1 | 56.4 | 69.0 | 61.5 | 68.5 | 55.4 | 46.3 | 73.8 | 68.7 | 42.6 | 59.7 |
| 1952 | 52.4 | 60.0 | 68.5 | 64.0 | 69.6 | 58.1 | 48.5 | 73.8 | 67.4 | 45.4 | 59.9 |
| 1953 | 52.4 | 60.5 | 68.6 | 67.5 | 71.4 | 61.2 | 50.9 | 74.8 | 67.7 | 47.9 | 59.5 |
| 1954 | 53.4 | 61.6 | 68.8 | 69.8 | 71.9 | 63.3 | 52.6 | 72.4 | 67.4 | 49.1 | 58.3 |
| 1955 | 53.9 | 61.6 | 68.6 | 70.8 | 73.2 | 64.3 | 54.0 | 73.4 | 68.6 | 51.0 | 57.8 |
| 1956 | 54.9 | 62.4 | 70.1 | 72.1 | 74.5 | 65.5 | 55.1 | 75.5 | 69.9 | 53.7 | 58.9 |
| 1957 | 57.0 | 63.7 | 71.2 | 73.4 | 76.4 | 68.2 | 57.3 | 79.0 | 72.4 | 56.5 | 60.5 |
| 1958 | 58.7 | 64.3 | 71.6 | 74.8 | 77.4 | 70.1 | 59.3 | 79.2 | 74.3 | 58.5 | 62.1 |
| 1959 | 60.4 | 66.6 | 72.3 | 75.8 | 78.9 | 71.7 | 61.2 | 84.3 | 75.1 | 60.3 | 64.1 |
| 1960 | 61.9 | 68.4 | 73.4 | 77.0 | 80.3 | 73.5 | 63.0 | 84.5 | 76.3 | 63.0 | 65.4 |
| 1961 | 63.3 | 69.0 | 73.9 | 78.0 | 81.8 | 74.2 | 64.6 | 85.2 | 77.4 | 63.5 | 66.3 |
| 1962 | 65.0 | 69.9 | 74.3 | 78.9 | 81.8 | 74.9 | 65.9 | 86.4 | 78.0 | 65.4 | 67.6 |

| Year | | | | | | | | | | | |
|---|---|---|---|---|---|---|---|---|---|---|---|
| 1963 | 66.5 | 71.1 | 75.1 | 79.7 | 82.3 | 75.0 | 66.9 | 87.1 | 79.2 | 67.7 | 69.1 |
| 1964 | 67.6 | 72.2 | 76.0 | 80.5 | 81.6 | 75.1 | 68.2 | 87.9 | 80.6 | 69.1 | 70.4 |
| 1965 | 69.2 | 73.7 | 76.7 | 81.3 | 82.0 | 77.8 | 70.0 | 87.3 | 81.0 | 70.8 | 72.3 |
| 1966 | 72.5 | 75.8 | 78.7 | 82.4 | 82.8 | 80.0 | 73.1 | 87.3 | 81.8 | 73.8 | 74.9 |
| 1967 | 76.2 | 78.9 | 82.0 | 83.9 | 83.8 | 82.1 | 77.3 | 88.6 | 83.9 | 76.0 | 77.3 |
| 1968 | 80.1 | 82.9 | 86.3 | 85.9 | 85.0 | 84.2 | 81.3 | 91.6 | 87.2 | 80.7 | 80.5 |
| 1969 | 85.0 | 87.2 | 91.2 | 88.7 | 86.6 | 87.8 | 86.3 | 93.6 | 90.5 | 85.5 | 85.1 |
| 1970 | 91.3 | 92.7 | 94.9 | 92.4 | 90.1 | 92.7 | 90.6 | 95.8 | 94.0 | 90.5 | 89.1 |
| 1971 | 96.0 | 97.0 | 97.9 | 96.6 | 96.0 | 97.8 | 95.1 | 99.2 | 97.9 | 95.1 | 94.3 |
| 1972 | 100.0 | 100.0 | 100.0 | 100.0 | 100.0 | 100.0 | 100.0 | 100.0 | 100.0 | 100.0 | 100.0 |
| 1973 | 108.4 | 100.9 | 103.6 | 104.4 | 107.5 | 104.6 | 103.9 | 101.6 | 102.4 | 104.9 | 109.0 |
| 1974 | 121.8 | 107.0 | 110.7 | 109.6 | 133.3 | 123.1 | 111.0 | 108.2 | 114.6 | 113.4 | 123.9 |
| 1975 | 132.4 | 115.2 | 115.1 | 115.3 | 150.8 | 130.3 | 121.8 | 117.7 | 130.0 | 122.0 | 136.0 |
| 1976 | 141.2 | 122.5 | 119.1 | 121.6 | 165.3 | 140.2 | 130.7 | 124.3 | 137.4 | 128.8 | 143.9 |
| 1977 | 150.8 | 127.3 | 123.7 | 128.8 | 182.2 | 152.0 | 142.5 | 129.6 | 145.1 | 135.5 | 155.9 |
| 1978 | 163.3 | 135.0 | 127.4 | 137.7 | 196.3 | 159.6 | 155.0 | 137.0 | 152.8 | 146.4 | 169.3 |
| 1979 | 181.5 | 144.8 | 132.3 | 147.8 | 226.7 | 188.8 | 169.6 | 145.1 | 163.1 | 156.8 | 188.7 |
| 1980 | 199.5 | 156.3 | 140.4 | 160.9 | 271.8 | 236.3 | 188.7 | 154.4 | 178.3 | 167.3 | 213.2 |
| 1981 | 217.4 | 168.2 | 145.4 | 174.8 | 307.9 | 260.7 | 212.6 | 165.9 | 193.1 | 179.8 | 234.5 |

# Chapter V

# *Fiscal and Monetary Policy and Inequality\**

## I. INTRODUCTION

The size and scope of any government in a modern economic system makes it very evident that actions by governments have profound economic effects on an economy. Public policy implicit in the governing laws of a society alters the economic position of individuals by its imposition of rules and regulations, which modify the operation of an economic system within a society. Governmental actions will affect not only the particular circumstances impacted by the scope of each separate law, but, unavoidably, the sum effect of these actions importantly affect variables at the macroeconomic level. Governments' ability to influence macroeconomic variables suggests an opportunity to target certain important aggregates as a national policy. They can pass laws to alter aggregate levels of taxes, expenditures, and transfers and thereby influence macroeconomic phenomena in pursuit of such a national fiscal policy.

While some laws establish rules, others establish decision units, which operate within a specified scope of operations to carry out some well-defined goals. The establishment of agencies clearly falls under this latter category of laws. The most notable example of these creations is the Federal Reserve System which has an

*This chapter is based on Russell, Slottje and Haslag (1986).

ubiquitous influence over the U.S. economy. It establishes broad policy for the control of monetary operations in the economy. So powerful is the Federal Reserve's ability to alter the operations of the national economy that monetary policy stands with fiscal policy as one of the two types of governmental policies most emphasized in macroeconomic analysis.

Whenever alternative policies for a nation are discussed (for example, to stimulate recovery from a recession), there is invariably a secondary discussion as to how the benefits of the policy will be distributed to various income classes. Monetary policy is sometimes argued as a more "neutral" policy vis-à-vis fiscal policy. Indeed, some political scientists are convinced that fiscal policy should be used purposefully to change the distribution of income. Despite widespread interest in the outcome of fiscal or monetary policy actions on the distribution of income, little evidence has been available to suggest the nature of the effects. Our study is an attempt to fill some of this gap and to estimate the effect on the distribution of income due to changes in selected policy-determined aggregate variables. We are especially concerned with those variables that are readily perceived as belonging to either the set of fiscal policy variables or monetary policy variables.

This chapter will analyze the impact of some fiscal and monetary policy actions on comprehensive income inequality. The model laid out in Chapter IV allows us to analyze and compare inequality in income component distributions with inequality in the marginal distribution of total income. Using this framework, various fiscal and monetary policies will be examined to see how they impact inequality across these income components as well as total income. Our approach is essentially a sensitivity analysis in that various combinations of fiscal and monetary policies are analyzed together to explore the overall impact on inequality in the comprehensive model.

## II. THE DESCRIPTION OF THE MODEL

Consider an economy that can be represented by a system of structural equations. More specifically, the economic system is defined as a linear model containing $G$ structural relations. The model determines the values of $G$ jointly dependent variables in terms of $K$ predetermined variables. The predetermined variables may be exogenous or lagged endogenous variables in the system. In either case their values are presumed to be known to us at time $t$. In matrix form the model is given as

$$By_t + \Gamma x_t = u_t, \qquad t = 1, \ldots, N, \qquad (5.1)$$

where $B$ is a $G \times G$ matrix of coefficients of current endogenous variables, $\Gamma$ is a $G \times k$ matrix of coefficients of predetermined variables, and $y_t$, $x_t$, and $u_t$ are column vectors of $G$, $k$, and $G$ elements respectively. Assuming $B$ is nonsingular (otherwise one or more structural equations would be a linear combination of other structured relations), $B^{-1}$ exists. The reduced form of the model is then

$$y_t = \Pi x_t + v_t, \qquad t = 1, \ldots, \qquad (5.2)$$

where

$$\Pi = -B^{-1}\Gamma \qquad (5.3)$$

and

$$v_t = B^{-1}u_t. \qquad (5.4)$$

$\Pi$ is of order $G \times k$ and contains $Gk$ elements. The $B$ and $\Gamma$ matrices contain $G^2 + Gk$ elements. While we may in theory deal with the set of income component variables as separately specified endogenous variables, it is not actually practical at the present level of our theoretical understanding of income component determination to do so within a model. Consequently, we relinquish this option and pursue a somewhat less ambitious course. We impose constraints on the income components under investigation by characterizing them by selected distribution functions from a selected family of distributions. Equation (5.2) shows explicitly that the overall model provides an explanation of $y_t$ conditional on $x_t$ and the disturbance vector $v_t$. What concerns us here, however, is that the underlying structure yields levels of income (etc.) which are observed and measured. If each structural relation $i$, $i = 1, \ldots, G$, is exactly identified (the necessary and sufficient conditions of rank and order are met) then for each reduced form Eq. (5.2) the comparative static analysis of a change in a predetermined variable to deduce the impact on the particular dependent variable can be pursued.

Clearly then, if values of total income and various components of income result from a general model Eq. (5.1), then changes in the values of the exogenous variables in the structural relations Eq. (5.1), mutatis mutandis, change the distributions of the values of these dependent variables in the system. The presumption made here is that an extensive mathematical model can, in principle, be formulated that treats the various income components as endogenous variables from which a distribution of total income may be constructed. Since we are concerned only with the effects on income distribution, the only endogenous variables in Eq. (5.2) of concern to us here are the various components of income. Our task, then, will be to examine how changes in predetermined variables of particular interest will affect the distribution of total income and the distributions of various components of income.

We discussed the choice of an appropriate hypothetical functional form to approximate the actual size distribution of income in Chapter III. Here we are concerned with the impact of monetary and fiscal policy on inequality in the various components that comprise total income. Thus a hypothetical statistical distribution, which allows for analysis across various income components is desirable. Again, a joint distribution function that allows this sort of examination and which is flexible to work with is the beta distribution of the second kind. Basmann et al. (1984a, 1984b), Slottje (1984, 1987), and Porter and Slottje (1985) have all demonstrated the merits of this functional form. By assuming the joint distribution of the various income components to be a beta of the second kind, inequality in the various marginal distributions (of each income component) can be examined. More specifically, in this study we wish to examine how changes in fiscal and monetary policy affect inequality in the marginal distributions of various income components.

Perhaps the most important characteristic of the beta distribution of the second kind is that the parameters of the marginal distributions sum to yield the distribution of total income (see Slottje, 1985a, 1985b). This allows for direct comparisons of inequality in the size distribution of total income vis-à-vis inequality in the various marginal distributions. Given these descriptions, we again utilize the joint distribution of the various income components are representable by the joint distribution function

$$F_{y_1, \ldots, y_n}(y_1, \ldots, y_n)$$

$$= \int_{-\infty}^{y_n} \cdots \int_{-\infty}^{y_1} \frac{K \alpha y^{c_1 - 1} \cdots y_n^{c_n - 1}}{B(c_1, \ldots, c_n; \alpha)[K + y]^\alpha} \, dy_1 \ldots dy_n \qquad (5.5)$$

$$y = y_1 + y_2 + \ldots + y_n, \qquad y_j > 0, \qquad \alpha, c_j > 0,$$

where $y_j$ represents the $j$th income component and $k$ is the lower terminal of the joint distribution. $a$ is called the Pareto parameter because, under certain conditions on $a$, the distribution becomes a Pareto distribution. The $c$'s are called inequality parameters for reasons demonstrated below. Inequality in any component can be analyzed simply by integrating out everything else. From the joint distribution function Eq. (5.5), the marginal density function of income component $j$ takes the form

$$f(y_j) = \frac{K \alpha y_j^{c_j - 1}}{B(c_j, \alpha)[K + y]^{\alpha + c_j}}. \qquad (5.6)$$

Again, recall the special property of the beta distribution of the second kind that the sum of the marginals of the various components maintain the same form as the marginal distribution of total income. Thus the marginal distribution of total income takes the form

$$f(y) = \frac{K \alpha y^{c - 1}}{B(c, \alpha)[K + y]^{\alpha + c}}, \qquad (5.7)$$

where

$$c = c_1 + c_2 + \ldots + c_{10} \qquad (5.8)$$

Equations (5.6) and (5.7) provide the necessary framework to study inequality between income components and total income.

As we noted above, while many measures of inequality exist, the Gini coefficient is intuitively easy to understand and is very popular (see Morgan, 1962; and Champernowne, 1974). For the marginal density function of component $j$ given in Eq. (5.6), the Gini measure takes the form

$$G(y_j) = \frac{\Gamma(c + \alpha)\Gamma(c_j + 1/2)\Gamma(\alpha + 1/2)}{\Gamma(1/2)\Gamma(c_{j+1})\Gamma(c_j + \alpha + 1/2)\Gamma(\alpha)} \left[1 + \frac{2c_j}{2\alpha - 1}\right], \qquad (5.9)$$

where $\Gamma(.)$ is the gamma distribution. Similarly, for the marginal density function of total income given in Eq. (5.7), the Gini measure takes the form,

$$G(y) = \frac{\Gamma(c + \alpha)\Gamma(c + 1/2)\Gamma(\alpha + 1/2)}{\Gamma(1/2)\Gamma(c_{+1})\Gamma(c + \alpha\ 1/2)\Gamma(a)}\ 1 + \frac{2c}{2\alpha - 1}. \quad (5.10)$$

The partial derivatives $\partial G/\partial\alpha$, $\partial G/\partial c$, $\partial G/\partial c_j$ are all negative, indicating that when $\alpha$, $c$, or $c_j$ increase, inequality as measured by the Gini index decreases. A natural way, then, to examine the impact of fiscal and monetary policy on inequality in the various marginal distributions is to ascertain how changes in fiscal and monetary policy variables affect the $\alpha$, $c$, and $c_j$.

## III. DATA AND ESTIMATION PROCEDURES

Data on the various fiscal policy measures for our investigation are taken from *The Economic Report of the President* for the years 1952–1981. The adjusted monetary base or "St. Louis" base is provided by the St. Louis Federal Reserve Bank. Data of total reserves, nonborrowed, and net changes in the Federal Reserves holdings of Treasury Securities are taken from the *Treasury Bulletin* (various issues). Both the narrowly defined money supply, M1, and real income data are taken from Gordon (1981). For this study, Internal Revenue Service data are utilized for the years 1952–1981. Ten components of income are analyzed in this study and these are given in Table V.1. By using group data techniques, the mean and variance of each income component are calculated from the IRS data which are given in frequency form. After getting the mean and variance, the $a$ and $c_i$'s are found by a method described in Slottje (1984). The Gini measures are calculated using relation in Eq. (5.6). The summary statistics for these are given in Table V.2. For example, the average measure of inequality in the wage and salary component from 1952–1981 is .333 and inequality increased in that component over time. The next task is to see how monetary and fiscal policies have impacted inequality levels across components and in the distribution of total income.[1]

To analyze the impact of these policies on the marginal distributions of income the following relation is conjectured:

$$c_{j,t},\ \alpha_t = \gamma_t \prod_{j=1}^{q} H_{k,t}^{n_k} \prod_{j=1}^{p} M_j^\beta j_t e^{u_t} \quad (5.11)$$

where the inequality parameters $c_j$ and a [so-called because of

*Table V.1.* The Components of Income Used

The individual components of income used were categorized in the following way:

1. Wages and Salaries (80.7)
2. Income from Dividends (2.7)
3. Income from Interest on Assets (2.8)
4. Income from Pensions and Annuities (2.1)
5. Income from Rents and Royalties (4.2)
6. Income from Business, Professions and Farms (4.3)
7. Income from Partnerships (1.3)
8. Income from Sale of Capital Assets (.9)
9. Income from Estates and Trusts (.6)
10. Other Income* (.6)

*Note*: The category Other Income includes categories such as alimony, state income tax refunds, small business corporation profits, and miscellaneous income sources. The numbers in parentheses represent the percentage of total income that each component composes from 1952–1981.

relation in Eq. (5.6)] depend on a vector of fiscal policies $H_k$ and monetary policies $M_j$. By taking the logarithmic derivatives or mathematical elasticities we have

$$ln\ c_j,\ ln\ \alpha = ln\ \gamma_t + \sum_{k=1}^{q} \eta_k\ ln\ H_k + \sum_{j=1}^{p} \beta_j\ ln\ M_j + U_t \qquad (5.12\text{a-b})$$

where $U_t = \rho U_{t-1} + E_t$, $E_t$ *iid* $N(0,\sigma_2 I)$.

Note that in Eq. (5.11a-b) could be specified to include a plethora of macro variables. Several studies have explored how some economic factors impact inequality [e.g., Muellbauer (1974)]. Consequently, we do not specify the model in Eq. (5.11a-b) to condition for other macroeconomic variables since many have been so extensively examined. Our purpose here is to analyze how fiscal and monetary policy affect these distributions. In order to explore the monetary and fiscal policy effects in a systematic way, we will proceed as follows. Different fiscal and monetary policy combinations will be regressed against all of the income components' inequality parameters to determine if these various policy combinations affect these various components in different ways.

By examining the impact of various combinations of fiscal and monetary policies on marginal distributions of income it is hoped

*Table V.2.* Statistics of Gini Measures

| Gini Measures of | Mean | Variance | Minimum Value | Maximum Value | Time Trend |
|---|---|---|---|---|---|
| Total Income | .324 | .00034 | .286 | .352 | Increased |
| Wages and Salaries | .333 | .0033 | .292 | .359 | Increased |
| Dividend Income | .703 | .0067 | .646 | .741 | Increased |
| Interest Income | .728 | .0074 | .578 | .874 | Decreased |
| Pension and Annuities Income | .864 | .0079 | .669 | .981 | Decreased |
| Rent and Royalties | .871 | .0015 | .798 | .926 | Increased |
| Business, Profession and Farm Income | .572 | .0013 | .503 | .663 | Increased |
| Partnerships Income | .733 | .0042 | .621 | .895 | Increased |
| Sale of Capital Assets Income | .768 | .0015 | .692 | .861 | Increased |
| Estates and Trust Income | .952 | .00043 | .883 | .966 | Increased |
| Other Income | .905 | .00082 | .841 | .958 | No Trend |

*Note*: The time trend was found by regressing the Gini measures against time with an appropriate adjustment for autocorrelation. This table reprinted from Slottje (1987).

that insight will be gained as to how the interaction of these policies may be achieving any redistributional goals. Obviously, it would be impossible to look at all possible descriptions of fiscal and monetary policies (as defined below). The sensitivity analysis is done on one fiscal policy variable with one monetary policy variable to try to isolate these effects on inequality. We realize that, changes in reserve requirements and open market operations may both simultaneously interact with nonmilitary government outlays to impact inequality. By examining only the sensitivity of inequality changes in marginal income distributions to reserve requirement changes and nonmilitary outlay changes or the sensitivity of changes in inequality in marginal income distributions to reserve requirement changes, and government expenditure outlays, the other interactions are implicitly accounted for. As will be seen below, the monetary policy variables analyzed are highly collinear, thus any one could serve as an instrument for the other, see Table V.3. Any attempt to incorporate more than one variable into the regression equation would cause well-known estimation problems. Furthermore, the high degree of correlation

*Table V.3.* Correlation Coefficients for the Monetary and Fiscal Policy Variables

Monetary Policy Correlation Coefficients[a]

|  | ABASE | FCHNG | NONBOR | TOTRES | M1 |
|---|---|---|---|---|---|
| ABASE | 1.00000 | .67351 | .97847 | .97662 | .99739 |
| FCHNG | .67351 | 1.00000 | .71491 | .70448 | .75870 |
| NONBOR | .97847 | .71491 | 1.00000 | .99864 | .98426 |
| TOTRES | .97662 | .70448 | .99864 | 1.00000 | .98239 |
| M1 | .99739 | .75870 | .98426 | .98239 | 1.00000 |

Fiscal Policy Correlation Coefficients[b]

|  | GEXP2 | GEXP | PGEXP | TRANS | TAXES |
|---|---|---|---|---|---|
| GEXP2 | 1.00000 | 1.00000 | .99691 | .99315 | |
| GEXP | 1.00000 | 1.00000 | .00690 | .99314 | |
| PGEXP | .99691 | .99690 | 1.00000 | .98947 | |
| TRANS | .99315 | .99314 | .98947 | 1.00000 | |
| TAXES | .99272 | .99274 | .98185 | .98532 | 1.00000 |

[a]Read as correlation between (say) TOTRES and M1 is .98239.
[b]Read as correlation between (say) GEXP and TRANS is .99314.

makes vacuous any attempt at gaining additional explanation power. The same argument holds for fiscal policy variables.

The estimation results are now given in Section IV later. A few comments on the estimation procedure, however, before we proceed. Actual estimation of the Eq. (5.12a-b) was done with Gauss-Aitken generalized least squares (see Fomby et al., 1984) to adjust for autocorrelation, which was detected. Reported below, in addition to the estimated coefficients, are the autoregressive parameter $p$ and a collinearity measure. This index is computed using an approach developed by Belsley et al. (1980). Only a subset of the 275 regression results are reported in Tables V.4–V.28 in order to reduce the volume of statistical reporting and to focus our discussion. The selection criterion for this subset is that we require at least one explanatory variable in a particular distribution of total income or income component specifications be statistically significant at a 10 percent level. We find that 126 of the total income and income component equations meet this criterion.

*(Text continues on page 118)*

*Table V.4.* Estimates of the Impact of Government Expenditures
and Changes in Adjusted Monetary Base on Inequality
in Various Components

| Dependent Variable | $\eta$ | $\beta$ | $\varrho$ | Collinearity Index |
|---|---|---|---|---|
| Model 1: $c_{it}$, $\alpha_t = \gamma + \eta GEXP_t + \beta ABASE_t + U_t$ | | | | |
| $c$ | $-.0004026^{**}$ | $.177705^{**}$ | $.1792$ | $76.59$ |
| $c_1$ | $-.0003044^{*}$ | $.136936^{**}$ | $.2197$ | |
| $c_4$ | $-.0000109^{*}$ | $.008354$ | $-.3127$ | |
| $c_7$ | $-.0000216^{*}$ | $.005798$ | $-.7024^{**}$ | |
| $c_{10}$ | $.0000191^{**}$ | $-.006825^{**}$ | $-.5372^{**}$ | |

*denotes significance at the .10 level.
**denotes significance at the .05 level.
*Note*: The collinearity index is a measure of the degree of collinearity among the independent variables. A value of the index under 30 indicates weak collinearity, between 31–80 indicates moderate collinearity. Over 80 indicates some problem may arise in inverting the $(x'x)$ matrix.

*Table V.5.* Estimates of the Impact of Government Expenditures
Less Military Outlays and Changes in the Adjusted Monetary Base
on Inequality in Various Components

| Dependent Variable | $\eta$ | $\beta$ | $\varrho$ | Collinearity Index |
|---|---|---|---|---|
| Model 2: $c_{it}$, $\alpha_t = \gamma + \eta GEXP2_t + \beta ABASE_t + U_t$ | | | | |
| $c$ | $-.000401^{**}$ | $.17666^{**}$ | $.1772$ | $76.638$ |
| $c_1$ | $-.000303^{*}$ | $.13614^{**}$ | $.2181$ | |
| $c_4$ | $-.000011^{*}$ | $.00836$ | $-.3121$ | |
| $c_7$ | $-.000022^{*}$ | $.005804$ | $-.7021^{**}$ | |
| $c_{10}$ | $.000010^{**}$ | $-.00684^{**}$ | $-.5375^{**}$ | |

*Note*: See Table V.4 for explanation of symbols.

*Table V.6.* Estimates of the Impact of Transfer Payments and Changes in the Adjusted Monetary Base on Inequality in Various Components

| Dependent Variable | $\eta$ | $\beta$ | $\varrho$ | Collinearity Index |
|---|---|---|---|---|
| Model 3: $c_{it}$, $\alpha_t = \gamma + \eta TRANS_t + \beta ABASE_t + U_t$ | | | | |
| $c_4$ | .01334* | −.00004 | −.4251 | 47.745 |

*Note*: See Table V.4 for explanation of symbols.

*Table V.7.* Estimates of the Impact of Ratio of Government Expenditures to Real Income and Changes in the Adjusted Monetary Base on Inequality in Various Components

| Dependent Variable | $\eta$ | $\beta$ | $\varrho$ | Collinearity Index |
|---|---|---|---|---|
| Model 4: $c_{it}$, $\alpha_t + \eta PGEXP_t + \beta ABASE_t + U_t$ | | | | |
| $c$ | .3744** | .09815** | .1469 | 46.43 |
| $c_1$ | −.26014* | .071801** | .1782 | |
| $c_4$ | −.004997 | .00501** | −.369** | |
| $c_6$ | −.02737* | .00174 | −.5382** | |
| $c_7$ | −.02155** | .00174 | −.7174** | |
| $c_8$ | −.02451* | .00588* | −.3880** | |

*Note*: See Table V.4 for explanation of asterisks.

*Table V.8.* Estimates of the Impact of Government Expenditures and Changes in Nonborrowed Reserves on Inequality in Various Components

| Dependent Variable | $\eta$ | $\beta$ | $\varrho$ | Collinearity Index |
|---|---|---|---|---|
| Model 5: $c_{it}$, $\alpha_t = \gamma + \eta GEXP_t + \beta NONBOR_t + U_t$ | | | | |
| $c_2$ | .000004 | −.01055** | −.3003 | 29.567 |
| $c_3$ | .00001** | .01273 | −.4494** | |
| $c_4$ | .00001** | .00744* | −.3885** | |
| $c_{10}$ | .00001** | −.0061 | −.4548** | |

*Note*: See Table V.4 for explanation of asterisks.

*Table V.9.* Estimates of the Impact of Government Expenditures
Less Military Outlays and Changes in Nonborrowed Reserves
on Inequality in Various Components

| Dependent Variable | $\eta$ | $\beta$ | $\varrho$ | Collinearity Index |
|---|---|---|---|---|
| Model 6: $c_{it}$, $\alpha_t = \gamma + \eta \text{GEXP2}_t + \beta \text{NONBOR}_t + U_t$ | | | | |
| $c_2$ | .000004 | −.01056** | −.3001 | 29.548 |
| $c_3$ | .00001** | .01274 | .4493** | |
| $c_4$ | .00001** | .007734* | −.3884** | |
| $c_7$ | −.000022* | .0058 | −.7021** | |
| $c_{10}$ | .00001** | −.00612 | −.455** | |

*Note*: See Table V.4 for explanation of asterisks.

*Table V.10.* Estimates of the Impact of Transfer Payments
and Changes in Nonborrowed Reserves on Inequality
in Various Components

| Dependent Variable | $\eta$ | $\beta$ | $\varrho$ | Collinearity Index |
|---|---|---|---|---|
| Model 7: $c_{it}$, $\alpha_t = \gamma + \eta \text{TRANS}_t + \beta \text{NONBOR}_t + U_t$ | | | | |
| $c_2$ | .00568 | −.011* | −.3317 | 37.118 |
| $c_3$ | .01585** | .00976 | −.4459** | |
| $c_4$ | .01166** | .0021 | −.4418** | |

*Note*: See Table V.4 for explanation of asterisks.

*Table V.11.* Estimates of the Impact of Ratio of Government
Expenditures to Real Income and Changes in Nonborrowed Reserves
on Inequality in Various Components

| Dependent Variable | $\eta$ | $\beta$ | $\varrho$ | Collinearity Index |
|---|---|---|---|---|
| Model 8: $c_{it}$, $\alpha_t = \gamma + \eta \text{PGEXP}_t + \beta \text{NONBOR}_t + U_t$ | | | | |
| $c_3$ | −.014901** | .015515** | −.4509** | 27.803 |
| $c_4$ | .007589** | .009675** | −.4042** | |
| $c_7$ | −.0166* | −.00353 | −.6082** | |
| $c_{10}$ | .007999* | −.00376 | −.4641** | |

*Note*: See Table V.4 for explanation of asterisks.

*Table V.12.* Estimates of the Impact of Government Expenditures and Changes in Total Reserves on Inequality in Various Components

| Dependent Variable | $\eta$ | $\beta$ | $\varrho$ | Collinearity Index |
|---|---|---|---|---|
| Model 9: $c_{it}, \alpha_t = \gamma + \eta GEXP_t + \beta TOTRES_t + U_t$ | | | | |
| $c_2$ | .000003 | −.0086* | −.3486** | 28.377 |
| $c_3$ | .000013 | .00741 | −.4731** | |
| $c_4$ | .00001 | .00702 | −.3991** | |
| $c_7$ | −.00001** | .00052 | −.6087** | |
| $c_{10}$ | .00001** | −.00661 | −.4694** | |

*Note*: See Table V.4 for explanation of asterisks.

*Table V.13.* Estimates of the Impact of Government Expenditures Less Military Outlays and Changes in Total Reserves on Inequality in Various Components

| Dependent Variable | $\eta$ | $\beta$ | $\varrho$ | Collinearity Index |
|---|---|---|---|---|
| Model 10: $c_{it}, \alpha_t = \gamma + \eta GEXP2_t + \beta TOTRES_t + U_t$ | | | | |
| $c_2$ | .000003 | −.0086* | −.3484** | 28.36 |
| $c_3$ | −.000013** | .00742 | −.473** | |
| $c_4$ | .00001** | .00701* | −.399** | |
| $c_7$ | −.00001** | .00052 | −.6086** | |
| $c_{10}$ | .00001** | .0066 | −.4694** | |

*Note*: See Table V.4 for explanation of asterisks.

*Table V.14.* Estimates of the Impact of Transfer Payments and Changes in Total Reserves on Inequality in Various Components

| Dependent Variable | $\eta$ | $\beta$ | $\varrho$ | Collinearity Index |
|---|---|---|---|---|
| Model 11: $c_{it}, \alpha_t = \gamma + \eta TRANS_t + \beta TOTRES_t + U_t$ | | | | |
| $c_3$ | .0204** | .00302 | −.4716** | |
| $c_4$ | .01184** | .00184 | −.445** | |
| $c_7$ | −.01268** | .00185 | −.6232** | |

*Note*: See Table V.4 for explanation of asterisks.

*Table V.15.* Estimates of the Impact of Ratio of Government Expenditures to Real Income and Changes in Nonborrowed Reserves on Inequality in Various Components

| Dependent Variable | $\eta$ | $\beta$ | $\varrho$ | Collinearity Index |
|---|---|---|---|---|
| Model 12: $c_{it}$, $\alpha_t = \gamma + \eta PGEXP_t + \beta TOTRES_t + U_t$ | | | | |
| $c_3$ | .01881** | .01139* | −.4747* | 26.191 |
| $c_4$ | −.008312** | .00892** | −.4162** | |
| $c_6$ | −.01604* | −.00465 | −.4492** | |
| $c_7$ | −.0145** | −.00012 | −.6336** | |
| $c_{10}$ | .00815** | −.00393 | −.4709** | |

*Note*: See Table V.4 for explanation of asterisks.

*Table V.16.* Estimates of the Impact of Government Expenditures and Changes in Federal Reserves Holdings of Treasury Securities on Inequality in Various Components

| Dependent Variable | $\eta$ | $\beta$ | $\varrho$ | Collinearity Index |
|---|---|---|---|---|
| Model 13: $c_{it}$, $\alpha_t = \gamma + \eta GEXP_t + \beta FCHG_t + U_t$ | | | | |
| $\alpha$ | −.00001** | −.0267 | −.3983** | 4.624 |
| $c$ | .000041** | −.0348 | .0478 | |
| $c_1$ | .000038** | −.03174 | .09 | |
| $c_3$ | .000015** | .00744 | −.3298 | |
| $c_4$ | .00001** | .00678** | −.195 | |
| $c_5$ | −.000003** | −.00141 | −.4721** | |
| $c_6$ | −.00001** | −.00125 | −.3052 | |
| $c_7$ | .00001** | .0069 | −.4049** | |
| $c_{10}$ | .000003** | −.00068 | −.4243** | |

*Note*: See Table V.4 for explanation of asterisks.

*Table V.17.* Estimates of the Impact of Government Expenditures Less Military Outlays and Changes in the Federal Reserves Holdings of Treasury Securities on Inequality in Various Components

| Dependent Variable | $\eta$ | $\beta$ | $\varrho$ | Collinearity Index |
|---|---|---|---|---|
| Model 14: $c_{it}$, $\alpha_t = \gamma + \eta GEXP2_t + \beta FCHG_t + U_t$ | | | | |
| $c$ | .000041** | −.0359 | .048 | 4.619 |
| $c_1$ | .00004** | −.03179 | .0902 | |
| $c_3$ | .000015** | .0074 | −.3299 | |
| $c_4$ | .00001** | .0068** | −.1948 | |
| $c_5$ | −.000003** | −.00141 | −.472** | |
| $c_6$ | −.00001** | −.00125 | −.3502 | |
| $c_7$ | −.00001** | −.0069 | −.4048** | |
| $c_{10}$ | .000003** | −.0007 | .4243** | |

*Note*: See Table V.4 for explanation of asterisks.

*Table V.18.* Estimates of the Impact of Transfer Payments and Changes in the Federal Reserves Holdings of Treasury Securities on Inequality in Various Components

| Dependent Variable | $\eta$ | $\beta$ | $\varrho$ | Collinearity Index |
|---|---|---|---|---|
| Model 15: $c_{it}$, $\alpha_t = \gamma + \eta TRANS_t + \beta FCHG_t + U_t$ | | | | |
| $\alpha$ | −.0212** | −.0229 | −.4034** | 4.595 |
| $c$ | −.0003* | .1369** | .2197 | |
| $c_1$ | −.0631** | −.0706 | .1516 | |
| $c_3$ | .022** | .0044 | −.3035 | |
| $c_4$ | .01271** | .00383 | −.2629 | |
| $c_5$ | −.00371** | −.00077 | .4919** | |
| $c_6$ | −.01557** | .00096 | −.3076 | |
| $c_7$ | −.01036** | −.00564 | −.3898** | |
| $c_{10}$ | .00326** | −.00085 | −.4106** | |

*Note*: See Table V.4 for explanation of asterisks.

*Table V.19.* Estimates of the Impact of Ratio of Government Expenditures to Real Income and Changes in Federal Reserves Holdings of Treasury Securities on Inequality in Various Components

| Dependent Variable | $\eta$ | $\beta$ | $\varrho$ | Collinearity Index |
|---|---|---|---|---|
| Model 16: $c_{i_t}, a_t = \gamma + \eta PGEXP_t + \beta FCHG_t + U_t$ | | | | |
| $\alpha$ | −.02594** | −.0274 | .3944** | 6.896 |
| $c$ | .06728* | −.0213 | .0303 | |
| $c_1$ | .0652** | −.02214 | .0745 | |
| $c_3$ | .02762** | .0072 | −.3662** | |
| $c_4$ | .01563** | .0067** | −.2337 | |
| $c_5$ | −.00444** | −.0016 | −.4638** | |
| $c_6$ | −.02035** | −.00048 | −.3198 | |
| $c_7$ | −.13362** | −.0065 | −.4206** | |
| $c_8$ | .00457** | −.00056 | −.438** | |

*Note*: See Table V.4 for explanation of asterisks.

*Table V.20.* Estimates of the Impact of Government Expenditures and the Narrowly Defined Money Supply on Inequality in Various Components

| Dependent Variable | $\eta$ | $\beta$ | $\varrho$ | Collinearity Index |
|---|---|---|---|---|
| Model 17: $c_{i_t}, \alpha_t = \gamma + \eta GEXP_t + \beta M1_t + U_t$ | | | | |
| $c$ | −.0002 | .0474* | −.01 | 59.989 |
| $c_1$ | −.0002 | .0401* | −.042 | |
| $c_3$ | −.0002** | .0063** | −.558** | |
| $c_4$ | −.000002 | .0015** | −.164 | |

*Note*: See Table V.4 for explanation of asterisks.

*Table V.21.* Estimates of the Impact of Government Expenditures Less Military Outlays and the Narrowly Defined Money Supply on Inequality in Various Components

| Dependent Variable | $\eta$ | $\beta$ | $\varrho$ | Collinearity Index |
|---|---|---|---|---|
| Model 18: $c_{it}$, $\alpha_t = \gamma + \eta \text{GEXPS}_t + \beta \text{M1}_t + U_t$ | | | | |
| $c$ | −.0002 | .0471* | −.01 | 59.928 |
| $c_1$ | −.0002 | .0399* | −.04 | |
| $c_3$ | −.00002 | .0063* | −.558 | |
| $c_4$ | .000002 | .0015* | −.164 | |

*Note*: See Table V.4 for explanation of asterisks.

*Table V.22.* Estimates of the Impact of Transfer and the Narrowly Defined Money Supply on Inequality in Various Components

| Dependent Variable | $\eta$ | $\beta$ | $\varrho$ | Collinearity Index |
|---|---|---|---|---|
| Model 19: $c_{it}$, $\alpha_t = \gamma + \eta \text{TRANS}_t + \beta \text{M1}_t + U_t$ | | | | |
| no significant cases | | | | 82.991 |

*Table V.23.* Estimates of the Impact of Ratio of Government Expenditures to Income and the Narrowly Defined Money Supply on Inequality in Various Components

| Dependent Variable | $\eta$ | $\beta$ | $\varrho$ | Collinearity Index |
|---|---|---|---|---|
| Model 20: $c_{it}$, $\alpha_t = \gamma + \eta \text{PGEXP}_t + \beta \text{M1}_t + U_t$ | | | | |
| $c$ | −.3093* | .0368** | .025 | 42.343 |
| $c_1$ | −.2326 | −.289** | .074 | |
| $c_2$ | −.0156** | .0012 | −.611 | |
| $c_3$ | −.0104 | .0038** | −.509 | |
| $c_4$ | .0025 | .0016 | −.212 | |
| $c_6$ | −.0366** | .0014 | −.535 | |
| $c_8$ | −.0283** | .0029** | −.372 | |

*Note*: See Table V.4 for explanation of asterisks.

*Table V.24.* Estimates of the Impact of Personal and Corporate Taxes and the Adjusted Monetary Base on Inequality in Various Components

| Dependent Variable | $\eta$ | $\beta$ | $\varrho$ | Collinearity Index |
|---|---|---|---|---|
| Model 21: $c_{it}$, $a_t = \gamma + \eta\text{TAXES}_t + \beta\text{ABASE}_t + U_t$ | | | | |
| $c_3$ | −.002 | .011** | −.593** | 42.898 |
| $c_4$ | −.002** | .007** | −.351** | |
| $c_7$ | .002 | −.007** | −.696** | |

*Note*: See Table V.4 for explanation of asterisks.

*Table V.25.* Estimates of the Impact of Personal and Corporate Taxes and Nonborrowed Reserves on Inequality in Various Components

| Dependent Variable | $\eta$ | $\beta$ | $\varrho$ | Collinearity Index |
|---|---|---|---|---|
| Model 22: $c_{it}$, $\alpha_t = \gamma + \eta\text{TAXES}_t + \beta\text{NONBOR}_t + U_t$ | | | | |
| $c_2$ | .001** | −.013** | −.241 | 28.857 |
| $c_3$ | .001 | .021** | −.405** | |
| $c_4$ | .001 | .01** | −.414** | |
| $c_5$ | −.0005* | −.0002 | −.689** | |
| $c_7$ | −.0001 | −.013* | −.510** | |
| $c_{10}$ | .0008* | −.004 | −.351** | |

*Note*: See Table V.4 for explanation of asterisks.

*Table V.26.* Estimates of the Impact of Personal and Corporate Taxes and Total Reserves on Inequality in Various Components

| Dependent Variable | $\eta$ | $\beta$ | $\varrho$ | Collinearity Index |
|---|---|---|---|---|
| Model 23: $c_{it}$, $\alpha_t = \gamma + \eta\text{TAXES}_t + \beta\text{TOTRES}_t + U_t$ | | | | |
| $c_2$ | .001** | −.013** | −.275 | 30.05 |
| $c_3$ | .001 | .015* | −.411** | |
| $c_4$ | .001* | .009** | −.424** | |
| $c_5$ | .0005* | .0002 | −.709** | |
| $c_{10}$ | .001** | −.006 | −.368** | |

*Note*: See Table V.4 for explanation of asterisks.

*Table V.27.* Estimates of the Impact of Personal and Corporate Taxes and Changes in the Federal Reserves Holdings of Treasury Securities on Inequality in Various Components

| Dependent Variable | $\eta$ | $\beta$ | $\varrho$ | Collinearity Index |
|---|---|---|---|---|
| Model 24: $c_{it}$, $\alpha_t = \gamma + \eta\text{TAXES}_t + \beta\text{FCHG}_t + U_t$ | | | | |
| $c$ | .007** | −.023 | .001 | 5.707 |
| $c_1$ | .007** | −.02 | .035 | |
| $c_3$ | .003** | .013** | −.229 | |
| $c_4$ | −.002** | .008** | −.23 | |
| $c_5$ | −.005 | −.002 | −.476** | |
| $c_6$ | −.002** | −.004 | −.258 | |
| $c_7$ | −.001** | −.01* | −.346** | |
| $c_{10}$ | .0004** | −.004 | −.371** | |

*Note*: See Table V.4 for explanation of asterisks.

*Table V.28.* Estimates of the Impact of Personal and Corporate Taxes and the Narrowly Defined Money Supply on Inequality in Various Components

| Dependent Variable | $\eta$ | $\beta$ | $\varrho$ | Collinearity Index |
|---|---|---|---|---|
| Model 25: $c_{it}$, $\alpha_t = \gamma + \eta\text{TAXES}_t + \beta\text{M1}_t + U_t$ | | | | |
| $c_3$ | −.003** | .005** | −.653** | 40.41 |
| $c_4$ | −.0008 | .003* | −.294 | |
| $c_7$ | .003** | −.004** | −.654** | |

*Note*: See Table V.4 for explanation of asterisks.

## IV. ANALYSIS OF THE EFFECTS OF MONETARY POLICY ON INCOME INEQUALITY

The Federal Reserve's major instrument of control over the economy is the regulation of the monetary base through open market operations. Changes in the monetary base alter the portfolio of commercial banks and induce changes in the money supply. While variations in the total monetary base arise from other factors in the economy (e.g., commercial bank decisions to borrow or U.S. treasury expenditures), it is generally accepted that the Federal Reserve can choose actions to dominate the movement of the monetary base. Thus it is not unreasonable to take the level of the reserve base as the exogenous variable targeted by the Federal Reserve in carrying out its monetary policy.

The monetary base variable, ABASE, is regressed against the inequality parameters for each income component. The estimation results for the marginal distribution of total income and all 10 of the income components, using ABASE as the monetary policy measure, are given in Tables V.4–V.7 and V.24.

For all but one income component, the sign of the monetary base coefficient is positive when it is statistically significant at the 5 percent or 10 percent level. The lone exception is a negative (but significant at the 5 percent level) coefficient for the residual income component, other income. With a positive coefficient, an increase in the monetary base increases the $c$ parameter of the distribution in question. As seen from Eq. (5.9), an increase in $c$ is consistent with a decrease in the Gini coefficient. Since this suggests that a decrease in income inequality, our result suggests that increases in the monetary base tends to make income more equally distributed. This is not to say, however, that this tendency is established for all income groups as the coefficients are not statistically significant for several income components. The coefficients are significant (at least at the 10 percent level) for 5 marginal distributions: total income, wages and salaries, pensions and annuities, sale of capital assets, and other income. As noted, the coefficient estimate is negative for other income.

Estimation of the impact of the monetary base on the inequality parameters is affected, of course, by the choice of variable used to capture fiscal policy effects in the same regression equation. An exception is the interchangeability of the government expenditures variable (GEXP) and government expenditures less military spending (GEXP2). The correlation between these two variables is so high that they are statistically nearly perfect substitutes. Consequently, models 1 and 2 yielded identical results and we will refer henceforth only to the latter model. When transfers (TRANS) is used in the regression equation as the fiscal policy variable, neither the monetary base coefficient nor the fiscal policy coefficient is significant for total income or any of the 10 income components, with the single exception of the pensions and annuities group. In the latter case, the fiscal coefficient was significant at the 10 percent level. Despite changes in the specification for fiscal effects, the statistically significant (at least 10 percent level) coefficient for the monetary base is positive whether we consider total income or any of the component groups with the exception of other income, as is reported above. When the ratio of government expenditures to real income (PGEXP) is used as the fiscal policy variable, the monetary base coefficient for other income is not statistically significant. But the monetary base coefficients remain significant at the 5 percent level for total income, wages and salaries, and pensions and annuities. For an approximation of the relative sizes of these components relative to total income, see Table V.1.

The regression results for the monetary base specification of monetary policy suggest that an expansive monetary program makes the marginal distributions of components wages and salaries, and pensions and annuities, more equally distributed as measured by the Gini coefficient. Whatever the effects of the marginal distributions of income for the other components we can also conclude that increasing the monetary base also makes the marginal distribution of total income more equal, (see tables of regression results).

An alternative choice for the monetary policy variable would be total bank reserves. One could certainly suggest that Federal Reserve policy is controlling these reserves levels. What effect do changes in bank reserves have on the income distribution? As reported in Tables V.12–V.15 and V.26 we see a few changes from the previous results. While earlier the monetary policy coefficient for dividend income ($c_2$) and interest income ($c_3$) were reported statistically not significant, we now find cases where they are. The effect of changes in total reserves on inequality in the marginal distribution of these two types of income is in opposite directions. Expansion of bank reserves makes income inequality greater for the marginal distribution of dividend income, but less for interest income. Why this should be the case is not obvious to the authors. Recall that when ABASE is the monetary variable the coefficient for dividend income is not statistically significant at the .10 level.

The change in the monetary policy variable does not affect the result for pensions and annuities. The marginal distribution of income for this component becomes more equal as total reserves increase. However, in the case of business income, $c_6$, and pensions and annuities, the monetary coefficients, which are positive and significant at the .05 level for ABASE, are not significant with the switch in monetary specification.

The consensus direction of monetary effects indicates that expansive monetary policy tends to make the distribution of income less unequal in the sense of the Gini measure. This conclusion is supported whether the monetary base or total reserves is used as the monetary policy variable.

It may be argued that the total reserves variable should be modified. That portion of reserves which are borrowed might be removed from total reserves on the grounds that the Federal Reserve's role in these transactions is passive, and borrowed reserves are more properly considered to be at the discretion of commercial bankers. That is, the monetary policy variable should be only the nonborrowed reserves (NONBOR). Considering further that the major action of the Federal Reserve in carrying out policy is through open market operations, it would also be reasonable to investigate this particular source of changes in reserves. Pursuing this latter suggestion, we specify changes in Federal Reserve holdings of treasury securities (FCHG) as another candidate to represent the monetary policy variable.

The results obtained from using the last two specifications, however, contribute little additional information about the impact of monetary policy on income inequality. Upon using again the varying specifications for fiscal policy effects we obtain the regression results reported in Tables V.8–V.11, V.25 and V.16–V.19 and V.27, respectively. The model using NONBOR yields results similar to those from the model using TOTRES. When the monetary policy coefficient is significant, we find it negative in the regression equation for dividend income but positive for interest income and pensions and annuities. But when Federal Reserve holdings (FCHG) is used as the monetary variable the only statistically significant cases for the monetary policy coefficients are for the pensions and annuities and the total income categories. These coefficients were positive. Expansionary monetary policy carried out by open market operations will decrease income inequality in the marginal distributions of both pensions and annuities income and total income.

As a final alternative specification for the monetary policy variable we select the money supply, M1. This variable is defined as all demand deposits and currency. This monetary policy coefficient is statistically significant at the .10 level in the cases of five different components of income and for total income. As the money supply expands, the marginal distributions of total income, wages and salaries, interest income, pensions and annuities, and income from sales of capital assets become individually more equal as determined by the Gini measure of inequality.

The monetary policy coefficient is insignificant for the component distributions of dividend income, rent and royalties, business, professional and farm incomes; partnership income; estate and trust income; and other income. It should be emphasized that while the monetary policy coefficients are negative for some versions of our M1 specification, in no cases is the coefficient negative when statistically significant at the .10 level.

The alternative specifications we use for the monetary policy variable do not alter in a substantial way the regression results for the monetary policy coefficient. This is not totally unexpected because the nature of the variables suggest that there should be high correlation among the variables. Indeed, this is the case we report in Table V.3. The monetary base, nonborrowed reserves, and the money supply variables are closely correlated with correlation coefficients in excess of .95. However, it is nonetheless useful to estimate the regression model with these different variables because the fiscal policy coefficients are affected by choice of monetary policy variable. We will say more about this below, as we discuss fiscal policy implications.

# V. ANALYSIS OF THE EFFECTS OF FISCAL POLICY ON INCOME INEQUALITY

## A. Government Expenditures and Government Transfers

A perusal of the regression results in Tables IV–28 reveals that an estimated coefficient for the fiscal policy variable of expenditures or transfers can be substantially affected by the choice of the monetary policy variable selected to interact with it. When the monetary variable is represented by changes in the Federal Reserve holdings of the U.S. securities, the fiscal policy coefficient in the regression equation for the inequality parameter $c$ is negative for transfers but positive for the alternatives, nonmilitary expenditures or ratio of government expenditures to real income. The monetary policy coefficient is statistically significant in the first case, but not in the latter two. The only other statistically significant result for the fiscal policy coefficients for the total income case occurs when the monetary policy variable is the monetary base. The coefficient is negative, and statistically significant at the .05 level when nonmilitary expenditures or the proportion of government expenditures to income is specified. It should be noted that this sign is opposite to what we report for the monetary base. Interestingly, in the two cases when the sign reversal occurs (due to change in monetary specification) the absolute magnitude of the negative coefficient is larger than that of the positive one, for the respective fiscal variable. Moreover, in and only in the case where the fiscal policy coefficient is negative and statistically significant is the monetary policy coefficient simultaneously significant at the .05 level.

The effect of the various nontax fiscal policy variables on the marginal distributions of income for the various components displays some uniformity. Where the fiscal policy coefficients are at least significant at the .10 level, some are negative regardless of the specification of the monetary policy variable. This result holds for the income components rent and royalties; business, professional, and farm income; partnership income; and income from the sale of capital assets. For each of these cases an increase in the fiscal policy variable makes the distribution of income within the group less equal. The result is especially robust relative to differing monetary specifications in the case of partnership income.

Only the model with the combination of transfers (for fiscal policy) and nonborrowed reserves (for monetary policy) does not yield statistically significant fiscal coefficient. The least robust in this sense is the case of rent and royalties income, where the coefficients are significant only when changes in holdings of U.S. securities is the monetary policy variable.

In every instance where the expenditures or transfer fiscal policy coefficient is statistically significant, the coefficient is positive except when the monetary base is the monetary policy variable. This sign holds regardless of our choice of nontax fiscal policy variable. This implies that increases in government expenditures or transfers tend to decrease income inequality for interest income and pensions and annuities income.

When the monetary base is used in the model, however, the fiscal policy coefficient is not significant for the interest income component. On the other hand, a negative and statistically significant coefficient is obtained for the government expenditure variable. The fiscal policy coefficient sign for interest income, pension and annuities, partnership income, and other income is invariant (when statistically significant at the .05 level) regardless of choice of monetary or fiscal policy variables. At the .10 level the only fiscal coefficient whose sign is reversed is for pensions and annuities income, and this occurs when the monetary base is used for the monetary policy variable. More surprising, for the pensions and annuities income component the government expenditures variable now yields a coefficient which is significant at the .10 level and opposite in sign from that obtained in all nine other cases where the coefficients are significant. With transfers as the fiscal variable, for example, the coefficient is positive and significant at the .10 level even using the same monetary variable, the monetary base. Changing the monetary variable to, say, nonborrowed reserves, and returning to the same fiscal variable, nonmilitary expenditures, the fiscal policy coefficient is significant at the .05 level and is positive. Despite the exception, the bulk of the regression results suggest that this distribution of pensions and annuities income becomes more equal as an expansionary fiscal policy is pursued.

For the largest component of income, wages and salaries, the direction of effect of fiscal policy is mixed. The coefficients are statistically significant in five versions of our model. In two cases, however, the fiscal policy coefficients are reversed in sign when the monetary specification is altered. That is, depending on the monetary policy variable specification, expansion of government expenditures or the proportion of government expenditures to income may increase or decrease income inequality among wage and salary earners.

## B. Federal Taxes

While the results are essentially the same whether the policy instrument is transfers or any of the expenditures variables, there is a distinct divergence of results when we consider taxing as the fiscal policy instrument. In particular, we observe a matching of the coefficient sign for eight out of eight cases where the coefficients are statistically significant when we compare fiscal policy actions of transfers versus expenditures. A comparison of coefficients' signs for the tax variable with those for either transfers or expenditures shows that there is a lesser agreement in sign, with five out of eight cases matching. Interestingly, the disagreements are in those instances where an increase in taxes and an expansive monetary policy both promote a more equal distribution for income. That is, either of these latter policy actions will make the income distribution more equal for total income, wages and salaries, and dividend income. In contrast, as mentioned before, expansion of either expenditures or transfers makes income more unequal for these distributions.

All fiscal policy variables have the same negative direction of impact on income inequality for the interest income; pensions and annuities; rent income; business, professional, and farm income, and other income components. Finally, the coefficient sign is ambiguous for partnership income as the coefficient is statistically significant in two models but of opposite signs, and it is not significant for sale of capital assets income, nor for estates and trust income.

In a comparison of the consensus results of coefficient signs for monetary policy variables with those for the tax fiscal policy variable we find that four out of five signs are in agreement. Both tax increases and expansive monetary policy promote equality in income distributions of total income, wages and salaries, interest income, and pensions and annuities. Equality in the distribution of dividend income is not promoted by monetary expansion but is by tax increases. For other cases, one or the other policy variable coefficients are not statistically significant, so meaningful comparisons cannot be made.

## VI. CONCLUSIONS

This chapter analyzed the impact of fiscal and monetary policy on inequality in the marginal distribution of total income and in the various marginal distributions of income components that comprise total income. By utilizing a hypothetical statistical distribution function that is flexible, we are able to compare total income inequality to inequality across various components. The form used is the beta distribution of the second kind. We then derive a measure of inequality for this distribution, the Gini index, and demonstrate how it depends on the parameters of the various marginal distributions. After deriving the comprehensive model, we next explore the impact of different monetary and fiscal policies on comprehensive income inequality.

Our findings indicate that monetary policy tends to promote a more equal distribution of total income and more equal distributions of component income, regardless of the fiscal policy variable specified to be interacting with the monetary policy. When the monetary policy variable is adjustments in the monetary base or various definitions of reserves, the regressions clearly indicate a consistent tendency toward decreasing income inequality. When the monetary policy variable is defined as Federal Reserve holdings of treasury securities we find no statistically significant effect on income inequality. Finally, changes in M1, which can be seen as a reflection of the interaction of all the monetary policy variables, strongly indicate that the impact of monetary policy on income inequality is to decrease inequality. The mechanism(s) whereby changes in money decrease income inequality is (are) unclear since changes in the money supply affect relative prices and cause distortions in different relative prices at different rates. The key to the decreasing inequality bias of monetary policy may lie with these price shocks. These are questions we leave for future research.

The impact of fiscal policies on income inequality should, of course, be easier to analyze since the redistributional aims of government are ostensibly quite clear. However, the results in Tables V.1–V.28 indicate that this is not always the case. The impact of fiscal policy on income inequality is contingent on which monetary policy the particular fiscal policy is acting in concern with, and varies depending on which marginal income distribution is under scrutiny. This result is itself important, however, for several reasons. First, it means that if the government decides on a particular course of action to decrease income inequality; by increasing transfers, and at the same time the government is pursuing a particular monetary policy; changes in holdings of treasury securities, the net effect may not be the desired one. Second, if again the stated goal is to decrease income inequality, then our results may be useful for a different reason. The sensitivity analysis presented here indicates that a very effective policy, ceteris paribus, would be to pursue expansionary monetary policy with almost any fiscal policy if (say) less inequality in the marginal distribution of interest income was the stated goal. In general, however, our results indicate that fiscal and monetary policies seem to work against each other, or "neutralize" each other in the sense that when the monetary policy variable is "significant," frequently the fiscal policy variable is not and vice versa. The message is clear. When the government decides to pursue redistributional aims, careful consideration should be given to the policy instrument chosen and careful attention paid to other policies being pursued simultaneously.

## NOTES

1. For instance, Bach and Ando (1957), Bronfenbrenner and Holzman (1963), Kessel and Alchian (1960), and Blinder and Esaki (1978).

# Chapter VI

# A Dynamical Adjustment Model of Macro Effects and Income Inequality

## I. INTRODUCTION

In the 1950s economists were confident that monetary and fiscal tools of public policy were quite sufficient to regulate macroeconomic activity. The consensus view was that fiscal policy was the more effective public policy and there was some doubt about whether monetary policy was effective at all. A more central question of the time was whether using fiscal or monetary policy was "better" for economic welfare. In the 1970s, as inflation moved to center stage to become a major economic problem, monetarists maintained that monetary policy was efficacious but fiscal policy was not. The relative importance of the two policies apparently switched positions for a significant number of economists. A potent role for monetary policy is alluded to by Friedman (1975). "I regard the description of our position as 'money is all that matters for changes in nominal income and for short-run changes in real income' as an exaggeration but one that gives the right flavor to our conclusions."[1] Being wiser after the 1960s and into the 1970s, economists found that the problems of managing fiscal policy and monetary policy had been underestimated. "It may well be that more has been promised than can be delivered with existing knowledge and instruments."[2] In setting the stage for their paper, Modigliani and Ando (1976) write: "After many years of sharp and sometimes acrimonious controversy between the monetarists and their sympathizers on the one hand, and the 'non-monetarists' on the other, over the effects of monetary and fiscal actions on aggregate income, some consensus seems finally emerging at least over what to disagree about . . . ."[3] (Emphasis ours.)

However unsettled the broad issue of the effects of monetary and fiscal policy may be, a narrower and politically more inflammatory issue[4] is whether the pursuance of monetary or fiscal policy can affect the income distribution, and if so, in what directions? The recent Joint Economic Committee report (1986) shows that in 1983 the top 0.5 percent of households possessed 26.9 percent of all wealth.[5] The historical record high in this share of wealth was 29.8 percent back in 1922. It is interesting to note that the 1983 figure looks very much like a break in the long run trend toward less concentration of wealth since 1922. Given the apparent shift in the distribution of wealth, there will likely be much attention focused on the shape of the income distribution.

In the last chapter we conducted a sensitivity analysis to see how efficacious various fiscal and monetary policy interactions are with respect to their redistributive effects. We found a preponderance of evidence favoring monetary policy. In a general way, the chapter suggested that expansionary monetary policy tends to diminish inequality of income distribution. But expansionary fiscal policy, more often than not, increases income inequality. Interestingly, this issue can also be easily embroiled in a monetary versus fiscal policy controversy of its own for the study concludes that the effect on income distribution due to one policy type action (e.g., monetary policy change stipulating a change in the money supply) depends critically on the type of action chosen for the other policy (e.g., fiscal policy change stipulating a change in government expenditures net of military).

The studies on this issue have thus far neglected to test for persistence of effects over time of any monetary or fiscal policy action taken. Economists are aware of the importance of such investigations and Creedy (1985) specifically urges that applied econometricians analyzing these questions be more concerned about the dynamical properties of their research tools. The aim of this study is to investigate how monetary and fiscal policies affect total income inequality when the model of study permits the impact of an action to be spread over time. In other words, policies which have redistributive ramifications in period $t + 1$ may also trickle through the economy to affect the level of inequality in periods $t + 2$, $t + 3$, etc.

To analyze these questions we again present our statistical model of economic inequality and demonstrate how changes in monetary and fiscal variables may affect the level of inequality over time. We present the model in Section II below. The empirical results are reported and discussed in Section III. As we noted above, the empirical results are sensitive to how we specify the interaction of the monetary policy variable and fiscal policy variable. Therefore, using the empirical results, we simulate the effects of two policy rules in Section IV.

Specifically, we simulate the time path of a distribution parameter under a rule which specifies that a fiscal or monetary variable grows at a fixed rate (or magnitude). Under the second rule, we hold the distribution parameter constant and simulate the time path of a policy variable. The simulations provide us with further insights into how these complex economic agents interact within a relatively simplistic analytic framework. We now present the model.

## II. THE MODEL

Consider an economic model which is represented by a system of $n$ equations with $n$ endogenous variables (denoted $y_t$) and $k$ exogenous variables (denoted $x_t$). In general functional notation the model is given as,

$$F_i(y_t, x_t) = 0 \qquad (6.1)$$

where $i = 1$ to $n$. Assuming the conditions for the implicit function theorem are satisfied, we may rewrite Eq. (6.1) as

$$y_t = f_i(x_t), \qquad (6.2)$$

where $i$ is defined as above. Within the framework described by Eq. (6.2) the endogenous variables include total income and each of its components. The presumption made here is that an extensive mathematical model can, in principle, be formulated that treats the various income components as endogenous variables form which a distribution of total income may be constructed. While in principle we may do this, it is not practical with our current knowledge of income distribution theory to do so.

Consequently, we relinquish this option and pursue a somewhat less ambitious course. Since we are only concerned with effects on the distribution of total income, we stipulate that the individual values of income classes follow the form of an appropriate family of distributions.

Clearly then, changes in the values of exogenous variables in the structural relations of a general model [as described by Eq. (6.1)], mutatis mutandis, change the values of the dependent variables in the system. Changes in income components imply changes in the characteristics of the total income distribution. It will be our task to examine this link between changes in some selected predetermined variables of particular interest and the distribution of total income.

To pursue the course of action outlined we require a specification of a family of distributions to use in characterizing the size distribution of total income. The selection must permit a determination of an appropriate measure of income inequality. To begin, any density, $g(y)$, chosen to approximate actual income data should be flexible and "fit" the data well (cf. McDonald, 1984; and Basmann et al., 1984a, 1984b). A distribution is said to be a good approximation to actual data if the sum of squares of error (SSE) is small (where SSE is defined as the sum of the squared differences between predicted frequencies and actual observations in each class). Flexibility implies that the sum of the marginal densities maintain the same distributional shape as each individual marginal density.[7] Given these criteria, the density $g(y)$ in our model is again specified as a beta distribution of the second kind (BII),[8]

$$g(y) \sim BII \left( \frac{kc}{b-1}, \frac{\mu(\mu+1)}{b-2} \right) \qquad (6.3)$$

where $m$ is the mean and $k$, $c$ and $b$ are the parameters of the distribution (see Chapter IV for the BII definition. The derivation of the parameters from the moments of this distribution is given in Appendix I). Next, an appropriate measure of inequality in $g(y)$ must be selected. Recalling Champernowne's (1974) criteria of what a statistic of inequality should actually measure, the Gini coefficient is chosen. For the BII form, recall the Gini coefficient defined as,

$$G(y) = \frac{\Gamma(c + b)\, \Gamma(c + 1/2)\, \Gamma(b + 1/2)}{\Gamma(1/2)\, \Gamma(c + 1)\, \Gamma(b)\, \Gamma(C + b + 1/2)} \cdot \frac{1 + 2c}{2b - 1} \qquad (6.4)$$

where clearly, the level of inequality depends on the distribution parameters. The limiting behavior of the Gini with respect to a change in each parameter is

$$\frac{\partial G}{\partial c} < 0, \quad \frac{\partial G}{\partial b} < 0 \qquad (6.5)$$

or as $b$ ($c$) increases with $c(b)$ constant, inequality in the distribution as measured by the Gini coefficient decreases. Given this characterization of income inequality, we can proceed to examine the impact of policy on income distribution.

Despite widespread interest in the concentration of income, the relationship between governmental policy changes and dynamical implications for the distribution of income has received little attention aside from our previous study discussed in Chapter V. It is the aim of this chapter to extend that analysis by investigating the dynamic character of the relationship between policy action and income distribution. We postulate that both fiscal and monetary policy effects on the distribution parameters are spread over a period of time. To capture the dynamic effects of policy on inequality, a distributed lag model is used. Specifically, it is assumed that a policy implemented in period $t$ will effect the size distribution of income in subsequent periods. Obviously, the number of periods imposed for the policy action to "die out" is a matter of model specifications. We use an Almon polynomial lag model (1965) with a quadratic lag structure and a four period horizon for our estimation.

The Almon polynomial lag structure can be applied directly to the equation,

$$b = \alpha + \psi B + Z\delta + U$$
$$c = \alpha + \psi B + Z\delta + U \qquad (6.6a,b)$$

where $b$ and $c$ are the parameters defined in Eq. (6.3)–(6.5) and in Appendix I. The vectors $b$ and $c$ are for the years 1952–1981 and are estimated using Internal Revenue Service (IRS) data from

*Statistics of Income.*[9] The data are for the IRS's definition of total income and the estimation procedure is given in the appendix. The $\psi$ matrix is made up of a particular fiscal policy measure (e.g., transfers, government expenditures on goods and services, or taxes) and its respective lagged values adjusted for the linear restrictions which are implied by the lag-length and order of polynomial. Thus, $B$ is the matrix of restricted least squares coefficients. These variables will be explicated further in the next section. The $Z$ matrix consists of the selected monetary policy variable and its respective lagged values adjusted for the appropriate linear restrictions. The monetary policy variables are chosen from economic variables under the control of the Federal Reserve. The first variable used to proxy monetary policy is the adjusted monetary base which we designate as "ABASE."[10] The others are the level of total reserves (TOTRES), the level of nominal money balances (M1), and changes in the Federal Reserve's holdings of Treasury securities (FCHNG).[11]

We can illustrate the formulation of our model with a quadratic lag structure and four period horizon using a monetary variable, say, ABASE, (in concert with various fiscal policy measures) as follows: Let the $\Gamma$ matrix in Eq. (6.6) contain any of the fiscal policy variables and adjustment variables which affect income inequality. The $Z$ matrix contains the ABASE variable (whose current period observation is denoted $x_t$) as,

$$Z_t \delta = Z_{t1} \delta_0 + Z_{t2} \delta_1 + Z_{t3} \delta_2 \qquad (6.7)$$

where the subscripts $ti$, $i = 1, 3$, denotes the row and column of the $Z$ matrix, respectively. To clarify, let us further define $Z_{ti}$ for $i = 1, 3$ as follows

$$Z_{t1} = x_t + x_{t-1} + x_{t-2} + x_{t-3} + x_{t-4}$$
$$Z_{t2} = x_{t-1} + 2x_{t-2} + 3x_{t-3} + 4x_{t-4}$$
$$Z_{t3} = x_{t-1} + 4x_{t-2} + 9x_{t-3} + 16x_{t-4} \qquad \text{(6.8a–c)}$$

Thus, the model actually estimated would be,

$$c_t = a + Z_{t1}\delta 0 + Z_{t2}\delta 1 + Z_{t3}\delta 2 + \Gamma_t B + U_t \qquad (6.9)$$

and similarly for $b$. To recover the lagged effects, we have,

$$c_t = \alpha + x_t\theta_0 + x_{t-1}\theta_1 + x_{t-2}\theta_2 + x_{t-3}\theta_3 + x_{t-4}\theta_4 + \Gamma_t B + U_t \qquad (6.10)$$

where

$$\theta_0 = \delta_0$$
$$\theta_1 = \delta_0 + \delta_1 + \delta_2$$
$$\theta_2 = \delta_0 + 2\delta_1 + 4\delta_2$$
$$\theta_3 = \delta_0 + 3\delta_1 + 9\delta_2$$
$$\theta_4 = \delta_0 + 4\delta_1 + 16\delta_2 \qquad (6.11a\text{--}e)$$

If $\theta_2$ were positive and significant, it would indicate that inequality (as measured by the Gini) decreases when the adjusted monetary base decreases. Holding the $Q$ variables constant, we use a quadratic form to allocate the effect of any policy action over four periods of time. In the empirical section that follows, we combine various monetary and fiscal policies and use Eq. (6.7) to examine the adjustment process, in order to see how these variables impact income inequality over time.

## III. EMPIRICAL RESULTS

The regression results reported in Tables VI.1–VI.3 make it clear that changes in the distribution parameters are not large. To better appreciate the nature of income redistribution implied by a "small" change in an estimated parameter we begin this section with an illustrative example. Let there be $i$ individual incomes $y_i$, $i = 1, \ldots, 50$. (We can easily generalize to 50 income classes by interpreting $y_i$ to be the central measure of tendency in each class.) We order these individuals from lowest income to highest level (see Table VI.A.1). Assuming general equilibrium, if total output of this economy is $2,147,000, the mean income level is $42,940. Now, consider a redistributive action by a government that doubles the income of the lowest quintile of income recipients (10 poorest individuals), and increases the income of the next 3 quintiles by 10 percent each. This action is financed by an imposition of a tax on the highest income earner, lowering the highest income by $55,050 or 2.5 percent of total GNP. In our example, $c$ changes with the redistribution from 12.6498 to 12.7838. This is a change of 1.05 percent in $c$. The Gini coefficients associated with these $c$'s changed from .5021 to .5000 for a change of 1 percent. While 2.5 percent of GNP has been redistributed, the income

*Table VI.1.* Coefficient Estimates of the Impact of Various
Monetary Policies Used in Conjunction with Government Expenditures
on Total Income Inequality

| Time | GEXP | ABASE | GEXP | FCHNG |
|------|------|-------|------|-------|
| t | −.017*** | −.0346 | −.0084 | −.004 |
| t − 1 | −.0211** | −.0391 | −.0066 | −.0035 |
| t − 2 | −.0123* | −.014 | .0054 | −.0924 |
| t − 3 | .0094 | .0409 | .0276*** | −.1769** |
| t − 4 | .0439*** | .1255 | .0599*** | −.2879** |
| | GEXP | TOTRES | GEXP | M1 |
| t | −.0092* | −.0704* | −.0172*** | −.0222 |
| t − 1 | −.0091 | −.0887* | −.0198** | −.0267 |
| t − 2 | .00004 | −.0549 | −.0077 | −.0134 |
| t − 3 | .0184* | .031 | .0191* | .0177** |
| t − 4 | .0459** | .1689** | .0606*** | .0666* |

***denotes significance at the .01 level
**denotes significance at the .05 level
*denotes significance at the .10 level

*Table VI.2.* Coefficient Estimates of the Impact of Various
Monetary Policies Used in Conjunction with Personal
and Corporate Taxes on Total Income Inequality

| Time | TAXES | ABASE | TAXES | FCHNG |
|------|-------|-------|-------|-------|
| t | −.0115* | −.051 | −.0078 | −.0156 |
| t − 1 | −.0143 | −.0581 | −.0078 | −.0376 |
| t − 2 | −.0086 | −.0213 | −.0001 | −.066 |
| t − 3 | .0058 | .0594* | .0153** | −.1009* |
| t − 4 | .0289 | .1839 | .0385* | −.1421 |
| | TAXES | TOTRES | GEXP | M1 |
| t | −.0029 | −.0442 | −.0081 | −.0064 |
| t − 1 | −.0031 | −.0511 | −.0092 | −.0075 |
| t − 2 | .0007 | −.0207 | −.0035 | −.0032 |
| t − 3 | .0043 | .047 | .0091 | .0064 |
| t − 4 | .012 | .1521 | .0286 | .0214 |

***denotes significance at the .01 level
**denotes significance at the .05 level
*denotes significance at the .10 level

*Table VI.3.* Coefficient Estimates of the Impact of Various Monetary Policies Used in Conjunction with Transfer Payments to Individuals on Income Inequality

| Time | TRANSFER | ABASE | TRANSFER | FCHNG |
|------|----------|-------|----------|-------|
| $t$ | −.0046 | −.0485 | .0054 | .0171 |
| $t - 1$ | −.0054 | −.0566 | .0074 | .0127 |
| $t - 2$ | −.0025 | −.0243 | .0062 | .0132 |
| $t - 3$ | −.0042 | .0483 | .0016 | −.0607 |
| $t - 4$ | .0146 | .1613 | −.0062 | .1297 |
| | TRANSFER | TOTRES | TRANSFER | M1 |
| $t$ | −.024** | −.0697*** | .0165 | .0128 |
| $t - 1$ | −.0304** | −.0669** | .0228 | .0135 |
| $t - 2$ | −.0191** | .0083 | .0188 | .0022 |
| $t - 3$ | .0098* | .1561*** | .0046 | −.0213 |
| $t - 4$ | .0563** | .3764*** | −.0199 | −.0568 |

***denotes significance at the .01 level
**denotes significance at the .05 level
*denotes significance at the .10 level

inequality parameter $c$ and Gini coefficient changed approximately 1 percent. Clearly, extensive redistributions in income with significant economic impact on individuals are consistent with relatively small changes in the distribution parameters. (Note: the actual $c$'s observed in the U.S. from 1952 to 1981 ranged from 11.4257 to 13.2708.)[12]

Results of the regressions for the model given in Eq. (6b) are reported for various combinations of specifications for fiscal and monetary policies. In Table VI.1 the fiscal policy variable is stipulated to be the level of government expenditures on goods and services (GEXP). In Table VI.2 the fiscal variable is the level of personal and corporate income taxes (TAXES). The level of transfer payments to individuals (TRANSFER) is the fiscal policy measure used in Table VI.3. Some governmental transfer programs are undertaken with the express intent to affect the distribution of income so it is of interest to consider this variable in the context of fiscal policy. The monetary policy variables are listed across the top of each table and they consist of these alternatives: the adjusted monetary base (ABASE), the net change in Federal Reserve's holding of Treasury Securities (FCHNG), the level of total reserves (TOTRES), and the nominal money supply (M1). The parameter estimates give the effect on the distribution parameter $c$ of any change in a policy variable. A change in $c$ implies an impact on the distribution of income as measured by the Gini coefficient. The statistically significant coefficients are marked with 1, 2, or 3 asterisks indicating the level of significance, 10, 5, or 1 percent respectively.

Calculation from both distributions tabulated in Table VI.A.1 show that the redistribution scheme discussed above decreases the variance of the size distribution of income, while keeping the mean unchanged. In the Appendix we provide formulas for computing the parameters of the BII, namely, $c$ and $b$. Our empirical analysis will focus on the distribution parameter $c$. Of course, the distribution of income is a function of both distribution parameters, $c$ and $b$. But we concentrate on the estimation of parameter $c$ because the direction of impacts are substantially in the same direction for both. For the 12 policy combinations discussed here, only 20 of the 120 estimated coefficients have opposite signs for $b$ and $c$. Of these 20 coefficients, 15 are not statistically different from zero. Note that a change in $c$ results in an increase in $b$, other things being equal. While the qualitative results are preserved in our analysis of the distribution parameter, $c$, it is clear that the magnitudes of these coefficients do not reflect the complete change in distribution of income.

## IV. FISCAL POLICY IMPACTS ON INCOME INEQUALITY

### A. *Government Expenditures*

The time distribution of impact due to government expenditures (GEXP) are presented in Table VI.1 and are shown in Chart VI.1. The current, first and second period lag coefficients are negative and the estimates for the three and four period lags are positive. This means that a given change in government expenditures will result in the distribution of total income becoming more unequal, in the current and next two periods, but subsequently, the effect is reversed and later, increases in government expendi-

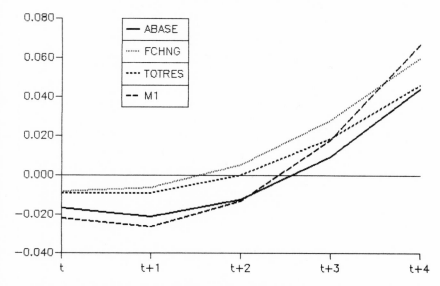

*Chart VI.1.* Time Paths of the Effects of GEXP on the Distribution Parameter with Various Monetary Policy Measures.

tures contribute to a lessening of income inequality. The general character of the distributed effects of government expenditures appears to be of this pattern regardless of our choice of the monetary policy variable specification. The immediate impact of expenditure increase is always towards increasing inequality. The total pattern of impact is consistent with a "trickle down" view. That is, government spending tends to benefit individuals in the upper portion of the income distribution initially but at later stages, those in the lower portion of the income distribution participate and benefit from the effects of policy. This latter decrease in inequality is suggested by the lagged positive coefficients. For ABASE, TOTRES and M1, the largest coefficient is positive and is observed as the fourth period lagged effect.

## B. Taxes

Interestingly, the impact of taxes (TAXES) shown in Chart VI.2 seem to repeat the general tendency reported for government expenditures above. A priori, it is not clear which way taxes will

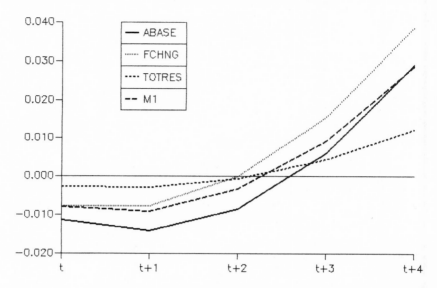

*Chart VI.2.* Time Paths of the Effects of TAXES on the Distribution Parameter with Various Monetary Policy Measures.

affect the distribution of income. For instance, an increase in income taxes, may have detrimental effects upon labor-leisure or risk taking decisions leading to slower economic growth. But a decrease in total income may have negative or positive effects on the distribution of income, depending on which segment of the distribution is more sensitive to the income tax. Our results indicate that an increase in taxes first increases inequality whereas later effects promote greater equality in the distribution of income. It may be noted that the impact of taxes on inequality is statistically significant only when ABASE or FCHNG are the monetary policy measures. We also specified models using an alternative measure of tax payments. With TAXES less TRANSFER as the fiscal policy measure, parameter estimates for the new tax variable were insignificantly different from zero when conjoined with any of the monetary policy measures.

While theory does not require that the effect of taxes on the distribution of income be in any particular direction the similarity of these results with the case of government expenditures may still be deemed suspicious. Indeed, it may simply be a reflection of a statistical rather than an economic phenomenon. Government expenditures are financed in large part by taxes and consequently, they are statistically correlated.

## C. Transfers

The results for the case of transfer payments to individuals (TRANSFERS) are given in Table VI.3. Transfer payments, it is sometimes argued, are designed to redistribute income from more affluent households to those in the lower end of the distribution. Chart VI.3 indicates that it is not clear whether the redistributive effects of transfer payments are currently working in the direction intended by policymakers.

The coefficient of the transfer variable are statistically significant only when TOTRES is the monetary policy measure. With TOTRES, the parameter estimates for TRANSFER are negative through the second period lagged effect, then the signs of the coefficients reverse in the third and fourth period lagged effects. This time profile for the estimated coefficients follows the same pattern as we observed with GEXP and TAXES.

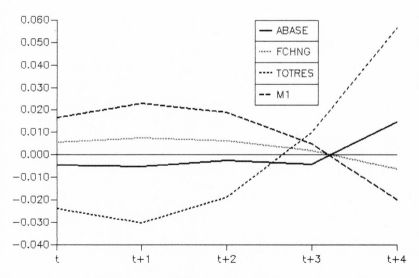

*Chart VI.3.* Time Paths of the Effects of TRANSFER on the Distribution Parameter with Various Monetary Policy Measures.

## V. MONETARY POLICY IMPACTS ON INCOME INEQUALITY

The effects of changes in monetary variables on the distribution of income can also be deduced from the estimated coefficients reported in Tables VI.1, 2, and 3. We will discuss the effects of a change in the adjusted monetary base, ABASE.

### A. Adjusted Monetary Base

It is seen in Chart VI.4 that the choice of the fiscal policy variable affects the coefficient estimate for the monetary variable. Yet with every fiscal policy specification the largest magnitude of a coefficient is positive (implying a decreasing level of inequality) and occurs in the fourth period effect.

With TAXES, coefficients are insignificant until the third period lagged effect, which is positive and significant. To the extent that an increase in adjusted monetary base is purely inflationary, price changes (with or without distortion) will impact inequality in

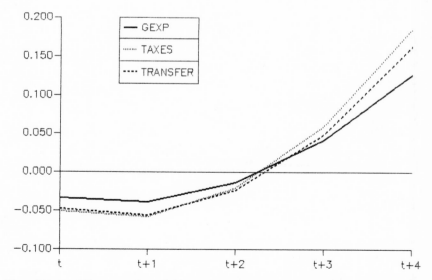

*Chart VI.4.* Time Paths of the Effects of ABASE on the Distribution Parameter with Various Fiscal Policy Measures.

an uncertain manner. This result has been well-known since a series of studies in the late 1950s and early 1960s (cf. Bach and Ando, 1957); and Bronfenbrenner and Holzman, (1963). However, if economic activity is stimulated and expansion in employment may very well decrease inequality.

## B. Federal Reserve Holdings of Treasury Securities

As shown in Chart VI.5, the results for monetary policy using FCHNG are similar using GEXP and TAXES as measures of fiscal policy. With TRANSFER, the time profile of the coefficients differs from the other two fiscal policy measures, but each of the parameter estimates are equal to zero (statistically speaking). However, the effect of a change in FCHNG is never statistically significant until a lag of three periods. When significant, the estimated coefficients are negative in each fiscal policy combination thus implying that these lagged impacts have adverse effects upon the distribution of total income. That is, an increase in Treasury holdings of securities promotes inequality in the distribution of

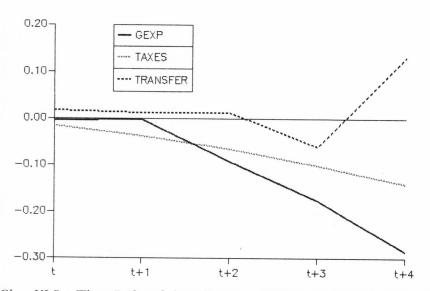

*Chart VI.5.* Time Paths of the Effects of FCHNG on the Distribution Parameter with Various Fiscal Policy Measures.

income. We should note that this is very different from the results we obtained for all the other monetary variables.

The observance of different results for FCHNG and ABASE over given periods is particularly surprising, in view of the role of open market operations in the management of reserves by the Federal Reserve. Buying or selling treasury securities implies a change in ABASE, other things being equal. However, transactions with the U.S. Treasury may explain some variation of results. Depending on the Treasury's timing in carrying out its operations the period effects of the two variables can be different. We note that, nonetheless, the total effect of a $1 billion dollar increase in the Fed's holdings of Treasury securities is −0.2388, which indicates that FCHNG, like ABASE, increases inequality in the income distribution.

### C. Total Reserves

Chart VI.6 shows that with TOTRES as the monetary policy measure, the most impressive statistical result (in terms of the

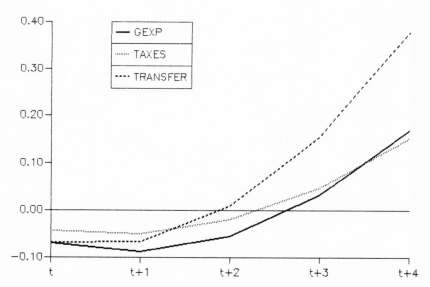

*Chart VI.6.* Time Paths of the Effects of TOTRES on the Distribution Parameter with Various Fiscal Policy Measures.

number of significant explanatory variables) is obtained with the model that uses TRANSFER as the fiscal policy variable. All the monetary policy coefficients, except for the second-period lagged effect, are significant at the 5 percent level.

## D. Total Money Supply

Chart VI.7 is the impulse response function for M1 as the monetary policy measure. The parameter estimates for M1 are statistically significant only when GEXP is the fiscal policy measure. In this regime, the third- and fourth-period lagged effects are positive and significantly different from zero. These results indicate that expansionary monetary policy reduces inequality in the distribution of total income.

Besides the results reported above, we considered two additional cases. We speculated that we might obtain different results by substituting a different specification for government expenditures. We tried total government expenditures both with and without military expenditures and found little difference in re-

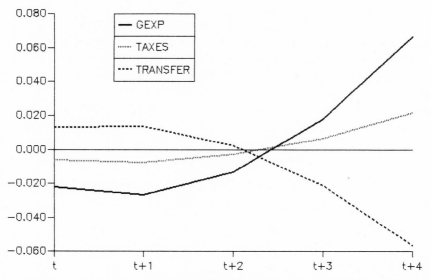

*Chart VI.7.* Time Paths of the Effects of M1 on the Distribution Parameter with Various Fiscal Policy Measures.

sults. A modification to remove trend effects of the government expenditures variable also yields no improvement. Finally, we considered the possibility that the level of economic activity might affect the relationships. Would the policy effects be sensitive to a given stage of the business cycle? We estimated each version of the model with an additional variable, a coincident economic activity index. Again, the results are essentially unaffected but do yield fewer statistically significant coefficients. The estimated coefficient for the coincident variable is statistically insignificant in every case.

## VI. TIME PATH OF THE EFFECTS OF POLICY ACTIONS

Existence of lagged effects suggests that the current effect of policy action on the inequality of income distribution may not be a good indicator of the final effect. Since the sign, as well as the magnitude, of a respective policy coefficient changes as the variable is lagged it is reasonable to explore two related questions: (a) what is the net effect of a one time change or rate of change in the policy variable over a selected time horizon, and (b) what must be the subsequent time shape of some designated policy variable after an initial change in policy if we require that income distribution be unchanged, i.e., maintain a neutral governmental policy.

Using coefficients estimated from our model and reported above, we can simulate movements of the distribution parameter over five periods in response to continuing policy action. Assume an initial long run stable position. For the current policy variable, $A_t$, we have $A_t$, and $A_{t-1} = A_{t-2} = A_{t-3} = \ldots = A_{t-n}$.

Lagging the regression Eq. (6.4) back one period yields:

$$c_{t-1} = \beta_1 A_{t-1} + \beta_2 A_{t-2} + \beta_3 A_{t-3} + \beta_4 A_{t-4} + \beta_5 A_{t-5}. \qquad (6.12)$$

The change in the distribution parameter is obtained as follows:

$$\Delta c_t = \beta_1 (A_t - A_{t-1}) + \beta_2 (A_{t-1} - A_{t-2}) + \beta_3 (A_{t-2} - A_{t-3}) \\ + \beta_4 (A_{t-3} - A_{t-4}) + \beta_5 (A_{t-4} - A_{t-5}) \qquad (6.13)$$

where $\Delta c_t = c_t - c_{t-1}$.

By our assumption, the change in distribution parameter as

described by Eq. (6.13) is zero. If a rate of growth, $x$, of the policy instrument is introduced only over the first interval then $A_t = (1 + x)A_{t-1}$ and substituting into a Eq. (6.13), we obtain an expression for the first period change in the distribution parameter:

$$\Delta c_1 = \beta_1 \cdot A_{t-1} \cdot x \qquad (6.14)$$

Over succeeding periods, we find two sources of change in the distribution parameter. In addition to the effects of an exogenous increase in the policy variable there is a persistent effect over succeeding periods (due to any earlier increase in the policy instrument).

Thus, for a change in $c$ over the fifth period we have:

$$\Delta c_5 = [\beta_1(1 + x)^4 x + \beta_2(1 + x)^3 x + \beta_3(1 + x)x + \beta_5]A_{t-5}. \qquad (6.15)$$

As observed from our reported results in Tables VI.4–7 the horizon of our model is five periods. Truncation after the 5th period implies that the number of terms in the bracket (in Eq. (6.15)) is limited to five. For additional future periods, we utilize a moving 5-period horizon. To illustrate for period six, we revise the expression in Eq. (6.15) to get

*Table VI.4.*   The Effects of a 3 Percent Growth Rate Per Year in Policy Variables upon the Distribution Parameter for Selected Fiscal/Monetary Policy Combinations

| Policy Variable | During Period | | | | |
|---|---|---|---|---|---|
| | *1* | *2* | *3* | *4* | *5* |
| GEXP | 16.9406 | 16.8308 | 16.718 | 16.7105 | 16.9741 |
| TOTRES | 16.9007 | 16.6846 | 16.3885 | 16.125 | 16.08 |
| TAXES | 16.8818 | 16.6246 | 16.275 | 15.9719 | 15.9442 |
| ABASE | 16.74 | 16.1869 | 15.5108 | 15.1113 | 15.6192 |
| TRANSFER | 16.8177 | 16.4106 | 15.8502 | 15.3454 | 15.2412 |
| TOTRES | 16.9102 | 16.7157 | 16.5354 | 16.5589 | 17.0875 |
| GEXP | 16.9454 | 16.8552 | 16.7943 | 16.8947 | 17.352 |
| FCHNG | 16.9945 | 16.9936 | 16.9819 | 16.9491 | 16.8817 |
| GEXP | 16.868 | 16.5909 | 16.2486 | 16.0371 | 16.2669 |
| M1 | 16.7412 | 16.1745 | 15.4376 | 14.881 | 15.0691 |

*Table VI.5.* The Effects of a 5 Percent Growth Rate Per Year in the Policy Variable upon the Distribution Parameter for Selected Fiscal/Monetary Combinations

| Policy Variable | During Period | | | | |
|---|---|---|---|---|---|
| | *1* | *2* | *3* | *4* | *5* |
| GEXP | 16.9044 | 16.7196 | 16.526 | 16.5039 | 16.9328 |
| TOTRES | 16.8374 | 16.4745 | 16.9705 | 15.5104 | 15.4048 |
| TAXES | 16.8064 | 16.3739 | 15.7786 | 15.2488 | 15.1664 |
| ABASE | 16.5701 | 15.6397 | 14.4854 | 13.7684 | 14.5477 |
| TRANSFER | 16.6996 | 16.0151 | 15.0614 | 14.1805 | 13.9487 |
| TOTRES | 16.8393 | 16.5264 | 16.2164 | 16.2396 | 17.1047 |
| GEXP | 16.9123 | 16.7604 | 16.6541 | 16.8143 | 17.5726 |
| FCHNG | 16.9942 | 16.9927 | 16.9731 | 16.9181 | 16.8041 |
| GEXP | 16.7833 | 16.3172 | 15.7331 | 15.3549 | 15.7037 |
| M1 | 16.572 | 15.619 | 14.3631 | 13.3817 | 13.6202 |

*Table VI.6.* The Effects of a 10 Percent Growth Rate Per Year in Policy Variables upon the Distribution Parameter for Selected Fiscal/Monetary Policy Combinations

| Policy Variable | During Period | | | | |
|---|---|---|---|---|---|
| | *1* | *2* | *3* | *4* | *5* |
| GEXP | 16.8138 | 16.4351 | 16.0194 | 15.9246 | 16.7246 |
| TOTRES | 16.6805 | 15.9383 | 14.8766 | 13.8472 | 13.4694 |
| TAXES | 16.6178 | 15.7338 | 14.4794 | 13.2898 | 12.9291 |
| ABASE | 16.1451 | 14.242 | 11.7936 | 10.0902 | 11.2812 |
| TRANSFER | 16.4041 | 15.0057 | 12.9972 | 11.0291 | 10.2504 |
| TOTRES | 16.6836 | 16.0422 | 15.3738 | 15.3359 | 16.9757 |
| GEXP | 16.8295 | 16.5175 | 16.2806 | 16.5638 | 18.0553 |
| FCHNG | 16.9934 | 16.9904 | 16.9509 | 16.8386 | 16.6027 |
| GEXP | 16.5715 | 15.6183 | 14.3801 | 13.4883 | 13.9993 |
| M1 | 16.149 | 14.2008 | 11.5471 | 9.3026 | 9.3718 |

*Table VI.7.* The Effects of a $1 Billion Change Per Year
in the Policy Variable upon the Distribution Parameter for Selected
Fiscal/Monetary Combinations

| Policy Variable | During Period | | | | |
|---|---|---|---|---|---|
| | *1* | *2* | *3* | *4* | *5* |
| GEXP | 16.9858 | 16.9675 | 16.9492 | 16.9494 | 16.9954 |
| TOTRES | 16.9246 | 16.7665 | 16.5515 | 16.3685 | 16.3544 |
| TAXES | 16.9835 | 16.9577 | 16.9233 | 16.8947 | 16.895 |
| ABASE | 16.944 | 16.8349 | 16.7045 | 16.6335 | 16.7464 |
| TRANSFER | 16.971 | 16.9166 | 16.8431 | 16.7794 | 16.772 |
| TOTRES | 16.9253 | 16.7887 | 16.6604 | 16.6882 | 17.0924 |
| GEXP | 16.9866 | 16.9716 | 16.962 | 16.98 | 17.0579 |
| FCHNG | 16.991 | 16.9835 | 16.8836 | 16.6068 | 16.0421 |
| GEXP | 16.9778 | 16.9408 | 16.8961 | 16.8705 | 16.9055 |
| M1 | 16.9728 | 16.9239 | 16.8616 | 16.817 | 16.839 |

$$\Delta c_6 = [\beta_1(1 + x)^4 x + \beta_2(1 + x)^3 x + \beta_3(1 + x)^2 x + \beta_4(1 + x)$$
$$x + \beta_5 x]A_{t\text{-}6} \qquad (6.16)$$

Since $A_{t\text{-}5} = (1 + x)A_{t\text{-}6}$, note that $\Delta c_6 = \Delta c_5(1 + x)$.[13] In general,

$$\Delta c_i = \left[ \sum_{j=1}^{5} \beta_j(1 + x)x \right] A_{t-1}. \qquad (6.16a)$$

When a policy variable is increased by some constant magnitude we can show that if the first period of implementation is $A_t = \alpha + A_{t\text{-}1}$ the $i$th period effect can be given generally as:

$$\Delta c_i = \alpha_i \sum_{i=1}^{5} \beta_i \qquad (6.17)$$

We observe that unlike the previous case, the change in distribution parameter is independent of the policy variable. The variable $a$ is mapped linearly into a change of parameter value by the sum of the estimated coefficients. That is, the term for $Wc\ddot{y}5\hat{\imath}$ is identical for every subsequent period because of our assumption of a five period horizon.

## VII. DYNAMIC EFFECTS OF POLICY ACTIONS

Using Eq. (6.13a) and (6.16a) we can calculate the results for several policy combinations. We choose to limit our discussion of dynamic effects to only 5 of 12 fiscal/monetary policy combinations to avoid much repetitive discussion.[14] Generally, the chosen combinations yield the best statistical results. Yet our selection was gerrymandered so that all of the three fiscal policy and the four monetary policy measures are represented. Five regimes, GEXP/TOTRES, TAXES/ABASE, TRANSFER/TOTRES, GEXP/FCHNG, and GEXP/M1, are used to examine four alternative policy actions. Three policies impose a constant percentage growth in the variable (3, 5 and 10 percent) while the fourth requires a fixed magnitude change of \$1 billion in the policy variable.

To analyze the dynamic effects of change in one policy interval, we assume that the other instrument is constant for a particular fiscal/monetary combination, or regime. Consider the regime defined as a policy mix of government expenditures (GEXP) and total reserves (TOTRES). To examine the effect of a new value for GEXP on the distribution parameter, we use the regression coefficients in Table VI.3 for GEXP when it is conjoined with TOTRES under the assumption that the latter variable is constant. The resultant values for the distribution parameter, $c$, for this regime and the others we investigate are given in Tables VI.4–VI.7. The values are given for five periods after an imposed policy change. After the fifth period, values of $c$ change according to the path dictated by Eq. (6.16). We chose the 1980 value of the distribution parameter, $c = 16.995$, as the initial value.

When government expenditure is the selected fiscal policy variable, with any monetary variables, we observe that a rise in fiscal spending decreases $c$ over the first three periods. The parameter bottoms out around the third or fourth periods to end upwards in the fifth period. There is a difference in the degree of the dip in value depending on whether the monetary variable. With a 3 percent growth in government expenditures the total decline in $c$ is $-0.285$ with TOTRES in the regime, $-0.201$ with FCHNG, and $-.8579$ with M1. The increase over the fifth period after implementation of the expenditures is 0.283, 0.458 and .23, respectively. Therefore, an increase in GEXP will result in a more favorable time path for the distribution parameter if FCHNG is the monetary policy variable than if TOTRES is in the regime.

The effect of changes in the monetary variable may be similarly investigated. With the FCHNG/GEXP regime an increase in FCHNG decreases inequality in each of the five periods. A similar occurrence arises with the TOTRES/GEXP regime. Finally, with M1/GEXP, the simulated distribution parameter falls through the first four periods and rise in the fifth.

The largest total impact upon the distribution parameter is observed in the GEXP/M1 regime. Through four periods, a 3 percent growth rate in M1, causes the distribution parameter to fall $-2.114$. The rise in the fifth period results in a total fall in $c$ of $-1.7538$. Moreover, Eq. (6.16) tells us that M1, conjoined with GEXP, will cause inequality in the distribution of total income to decrease in period 6 and all periods thereafter.

In TRANSFER/TOTRES, there are two noteworthy points. First, Table VI.4 shows that a 3 percent growth rate in transfer payments results in the distribution parameter falling in each of the five periods. Thus, our simulations indicate that transfer payments are not effective in reducing income inequality.

Second, the effects of monetary policy using TOTRES as the measure differs when TRANSFER and GEXP are the fiscal policy measures. With TRANSFER, the distribution parameter falls in the first four periods and rises in the fifth period of the simulated TOTRES policy. However, with GEXP, we observe that $c$ falls in each of the five periods due a policy involving TOTRES. Note that if we set the coefficients equal to zero when the null hypothesis that the parameter estimates are equal to zero cannot be rejected, the simulated time paths for the distribution parameter exhibit an increase in $c$ by the fourth period.

## VIII. NEUTRAL INCOME DISTRIBUTION POLICY

### A. *Single Instrument Neutrality*

In this section, the choice of monetary or fiscal policy values is made on the basis of explicit criteria. In particular, the values of fiscal and monetary policy measures will be presumed to be selected by policymakers in response to some initial disturbance in order to accomplish some objective. Suppose there is an exogenous increase in a policy variable. This implies induced changes in income inequality over successive intervals. At any point in time beyond the initial period, we can imagine some countervailing policy action which might be instituted to "neutralize" any further changes otherwise induced in the income distribution. Thus, a policy to be called Neutral After Period $j$ (nap $j$) is one such that $j$ periods after an initial change in a policy variable, a policymaker takes countering action using some policy variable at time $j$. The change in any policy measure between two periods depends on; (1) the regression coefficients; (2) the past values of changes in the policy variable before period $j$; and (3) in the case of percentage growth policy, the past values of policy variables. We shall derive two alternative policy actions for neutrality.

We proceed by deriving analytical solutions, for absolute changes and percentage changes in a designated policy variable. It is still assumed that the original state is a zero-growth path. Our illustration will be for $j = 3$, i.e., the case of nap 3. According to our definition of third-period neutrality, $\alpha_1 = \alpha_2 = \alpha_3$ for the absolute magnitude changes in a policy variable. Changes in the distribution parameter for the fourth period is given by

$$\Delta c_4 = (\beta_4 + \beta_3 + \beta_2)\alpha_1 + \beta_1\alpha_4 \tag{6.18}$$

and the requirement of nap 3 implies $\Delta c_4 = -(\Delta c_3 + \Delta c_2 + \Delta c_1)$. From these expressions the change in magnitude in the distribution parameter which must be offset in the fourth period can be determined. Substituting for $\Delta c_i$, $i = 1, 2, 3, 4$ into Eq. (6.17) and solving for $\alpha_4$ in Eq. (6.18) yields

$$\alpha_4 = \frac{\alpha_1\beta_1 + \alpha_1(\beta_1 + \beta_2)\alpha_1(\beta_1 + \beta_2 + \beta_3) - \alpha_1(\beta_4 + \beta_3 + \beta_2)}{\beta_1} \tag{6.19}$$

By the definition of $\alpha_4$, the value of the policy variable in the fourth period is equal to $\alpha_4 + A_3 = A_4$.

For the fifth period, neutrality is maintained if

$$\alpha_5 = \frac{(\beta_5 + \beta_4 + \beta_3)\alpha_1 + \beta_2\alpha_4}{\beta_1} \tag{6.20}$$

and

$$\Delta c_5 = (\beta_5 + \beta_4 + \beta_3)\alpha_1 + \beta_2\alpha_4 + \beta_1\alpha_5 = 0. \qquad (6.21)$$

Note that the solution for $\alpha_5$ depends on $\alpha_4$ and $\alpha_1$ and $A_5 = \alpha_5 + A_4$.

If the growth rate of the policy variable is in percentage terms, third-period neutrality implies $x_1 = x_2 = x_3$, $i = 1, 2, 3$ denotes the percentage growth rates. Consequently, the changes in the distribution for the first three periods are given by

$$\Delta c_1 = \beta_1 x_1 A_0 \qquad (6.22)$$

$$\Delta c_2 = (\beta_2 A_0 + \beta_1 A_1)x_1 \qquad (6.23)$$

$$\Delta c_3 = (\beta_3 A_0 + \beta_2 A_1 + \beta_1/A_2)x_1 \qquad (6.24)$$

and the growth rate implied in the policy variable for nap 3 are

$$x_5 = \frac{(\beta_5 A_0 + \beta_4 A_1 + \beta_3 A_2)x_1 + \beta_2 A_3 x_4}{\beta_1 A_4} \qquad (6.25)$$

Different terms to neutrality are easily found. Nap 1, for example, simply implies $\Delta c\ddot{y}2\grave{\imath} = -\Delta c_1$, and $\Delta c_3 = \Delta c_4 = \ldots = 0$. The policymaker must choose different time paths for the policy variables depending on their choice of the period to neutrality. After the $j$th period when the original income distribution parameter returns to its original value, the policymaker must continue to regulate the policy variable in order to sustain the parameter value, i.e., maintain neutrality.

We simulate an absolute magnitude policy regime of a $1 billion change per year in the policy variable and a 3 percent growth rate policy path for first and third period neutrality and report the results in Tables VI.8 and 9. Given each type of shock we determine the required path of a policy variable for selected fiscal-monetary regimes. The simulation results are reported covering 10 periods.

From Tables VI.8 and VI.9 we observe a marked swing in the policy variable for each monetary and fiscal policy measure. A neutral policy in our model imposes erratic dynamic movements in the policy instrument. After restoration of the original income distribution (i.e., in a neutrality "maintenance" range) the changes in the policy variable to be implemented by the pol-

Table VI.8. Single Policy Action Time Paths for Selected Fiscal and Monetary Policy Combinations under Third-Period Neutrality and Absolute Magnitude Policy of $1 Billion Change Per Period

| Time | GEXP | TOTRES | TAXES | ABASE | TRANSFER | TOTRES | GEXP | FCHNG | GEXP | M1 |
|---|---|---|---|---|---|---|---|---|---|---|
| t | 197.0 | 44.674 | 328.0 | 166.648 | 246.2 | 44.674 | 197.0 | 3.9 | 197.0 | 381.1 |
| t + 1 | 198.0 | 45.674 | 329.0 | 167.648 | 247.2 | 45.674 | 198.0 | 4.9 | 198.0 | 382.1 |
| t + 2 | 199.0 | 46.674 | 330.0 | 168.648 | 248.2 | 46.674 | 199.0 | 5.9 | 199.0 | 383.1 |
| t + 3 | 200.0 | 47.674 | 331.0 | 169.648 | 249.2 | 47.674 | 200.0 | 6.9 | 200.0 | 384.1 |
| t + 4 | 194.011 | 42.974 | 326.252 | 164.344 | 244.525 | 41.475 | 192.929 | 47.25 | 192.929 | 379.1 |
| t + 5 | 206.928 | 50.956 | 334.426 | 174.739 | 252.405 | 55.184 | 209.544 | 27.356 | 209.544 | 388.307 |
| t + 6 | 201.114 | 47.404 | 330.83 | 169.883 | 248.898 | 48.927 | 202.36 | − 1022.36 | 202.36 | 384.307 |
| t + 7 | 199.932 | 45.984 | 329.307 | 168.502 | 247.506 | 48.081 | 202.582 | 1937.66 | 202.5 | 382.626 |
| t + 8 | 197.031 | 42.781 | 326.08 | 165.085 | 244.31 | 45.373 | 201.957 | 24851.1 | 201.957 | 379.249 |
| t + 9 | 252.715 | 65.509 | 349.958 | 201.382 | 266.519 | 107.893 | 297.471 | − 11415.1 | 297.471 | 408.396 |
| t + 10 | 166.252 | 30.224 | 312.876 | 142.339 | 232.137 | 11.878 | 171.522 | −575458.0 | 171.522 | 361.47 |

Table VI.9. Single Policy Action Time Paths for Selected Fiscal and Monetary Policy Combinations under First-Period Neutrality and Absolute Magnitude Growth Policy of $1 Billion

| Time | GEXP | TOTRES | TAXES | ABASE | TRANSFER | TOTRES | GEXP | FCHNG | GEXP | M1 |
|---|---|---|---|---|---|---|---|---|---|---|
| $t$ | 197.0 | 44.674 | 328.0 | 166.648 | 246.2 | 44.674 | 197.0 | 3.9 | 197.0 | 381.1 |
| $t+1$ | 198.0 | 45.675 | 329.0 | 167.648 | 247.2 | 45.674 | 198.0 | 4.9 | 198.0 | 382.1 |
| $t+2$ | 196.011 | 43.414 | 326.757 | 165.509 | 244.933 | 43.712 | 196.214 | 3.025 | 196.214 | 379.897 |
| $t+3$ | 197.983 | 45.482 | 328.798 | 167.528 | 247.009 | 45.714 | 198.26 | — 18.434 | 198.26 | 381.943 |
| $t+4$ | 198.024 | 45.079 | 328.441 | 167.286 | 246.592 | 45.801 | 198.79 | — 0.57 | 198.79 | 381.61 |
| $t+5$ | 199.003 | 45.378 | 328.74 | 167.833 | 246.888 | 46.967 | 200.953 | 490.457 | 200.953 | 382.02 |
| $t+6$ | 192.054 | 40.804 | 324.028 | 161.949 | 242.375 | 39.754 | 193.583 | 732.134 | 193.583 | 376.75 |
| $t+7$ | 208.851 | 51.117 | 334.615 | 175.423 | 252.554 | 57.811 | 217.095 | -10067.6 | 217.095 | 388.711 |
| $t+8$ | 194.369 | 40.856 | 324.227 | 162.294 | 242.396 | 42.699 | 204.769 | -29202.0 | 204.769 | 376.833 |
| $t+9$ | 199.754 | 44.444 | 327.6 | 166.743 | 246.014 | 49.498 | 220.773 | 190984.0 | 220.773 | 380.928 |
| $t+10$ | 193.291 | 41.493 | 324.672 | 161.635 | 243.084 | 42.660 | 224.977 | 900549.0 | 224.977 | 376.902 |

icymaker is relatively small for the first few periods after policy actions. For instance, the required change between two periods in total reserves is never greater than $19 billion. Yet, the period to period swings appear to increase the level of total reserves then decrease. These changes may be quite substantial relative to the quantity of total reserves. Six periods after the initial policy action the counter balancing change in total reserves is $18 billion, which is roughly 46 percent of the quantity of total reserves in period $t +$ 6. Moreover, in the following period the required change is $-\$15$ billion, which is approximately a 26 percent decline in total reserves during period $t + 7$. This result suggests that policymakers must forego other stabilization goals if a target income distribution is to be maintained. There is a trade-off between maintaining a target income distribution and any other macroeconomic goals policymakers may desire.

Consider, for example, that policymakers' only other policy goal (besides a target level of income distribution) is to maintain some level of aggregate demand. As can be seen from our results, using fiscal policy, as measured by government expenditures of goods and services, to stimulate economic activity for 3 periods (under nap 3 for instance), will adversely affect the distribution of income. That is, the income distribution becomes more unequal. To restore the "original" value of the distribution parameter, the policymaker must change his target from maintenance of aggregate demand to maintenance of income equality. At first, the costs of changing from GNP as the policy target to the distribution parameter appear to be small. This is because the decrease in the fiscal policy measures are small in magnitude over the first few periods. In fact, for taxes, this small magnitude decrease stimulates aggregate demand. The gyrations exhibited in later periods with the distribution parameter as the policy target, correspond to excessively stimulative (for example, when government expenditures increase from $201 billion to $297 billion in one period in the GEXP/M1 regime) to depressing in the net period (e.g., the decrease in GEXP from $297 billion to $171 in one period). For fiscal policy, if stable stimulative fiscal policy is desired, our results indicate that income inequality is sacrificed. Switching to the income inequality target requires greater volatility in the control of fiscal policy variables.

In the same way a neutral distribution policy may be pursued using a monetary variable. Nap 1 and nap 3 are correspondingly calculated and presented in Tables VI.8 and VI.9. The volatility exhibited by the monetary and reserve aggregates under the two policies of neutrality imposes a cost to choosing a neutral policy for income distribution. This target implies the loss of a stable growth in the money supply. Moreover, the gyrations in the monetary and reserves aggregates are so severe (see Table VI.8) that we would expect interest rates to change substantially between periods in response to the required changes in the monetary aggregates. For example, when the money supply increases by a large amount (e.g., ABASE from approximately $162 billion to $175 billion income period) decreases in the interest rate may occur and aggregate demand may be stimulated. Yet, in the next period when the money supply decreases (e.g., ABASE goes from $175 billion to $162 billion in the net period), a reversal of the interest rate depresses aggregate demand.[15] Hence, a steady GNP target must be sacrificed in order to maintain some target inequality, measure of income distribution.

### B. Compensating Monetary Policies for Neutrality

With a modification of the previous section we can address ourselves to a different question. When a fiscal policy action is taken at the initial position, we have found that the distribution of income is affected over the first and subsequent periods. If policymakers are not pleased with the changes in distribution of income induced through some required fiscal policy action they might consider a compensating strategy. They may contemplate a coordinated monetary policy which could offset the redistributive effect. By judicious choice of a time path for a monetary variable they can effect the return and maintenance of the measure of income inequality to exactly the value it had prior to the fiscal action. In the light of the wide swings we observed earlier in the context of establishing neutrality we shall see that stability of an inequality measure requires corresponding wide swings in magnitude of the monetary instrument whether the initiating change in policy variable is monetary or fiscal.

In Tables VI.10–13, we report the results from a compensating monetary policy. We assume a one-shot change in a fiscal policy variable and consider the neutralizing action to occur after *j*

Table VI.10. Time Paths for Accommodative Monetary Policy
given Fiscal Policy Regime Change and First-Period Neutrality

| Time | TOTRES/GEXP | ABASE/TAXES | TOTRES/TRANSFER | FCHNG/GEXP | M1/GEXP |
|---|---|---|---|---|---|
| $t$ | 44.674 | 166.648 | 44.674 | 3.9 | 381.1 |
| $t+1$ | 44.674 | 166.648 | 44.674 | 3.9 | 381.1 |
| $t+2$ | 44.414 | 166.142 | 43.894 | 0.15 | 379.433 |
| $t+3$ | 44.742 | 166.55 | 44.369 | 4.781 | 381.091 |
| $t+4$ | 44.792 | 166.41 | 43.960 | 94.254 | 380.964 |
| $t+5$ | 45.011 | 166.376 | 43.469 | 89.802 | 381.517 |
| $t+6$ | 44.218 | 165.241 | 40.741 | − 1908.03 | 377.25 |
| $t+7$ | 45.856 | 167.873 | 44.952 | − 4347.36 | 386.92 |
| $t+8$ | 44.539 | 165.146 | 39.154 | 45473.7 | 377.959 |
| $t+9$ | 45.094 | 165.523 | 36.456 | 146903.0 | 381.157 |
| $t+10$ | 44.241 | 164.917 | 33.056 | −841042.0 | 377.628 |

156

*Table VI.11.* Time Paths for Accommodative Monetary Policy
given Fiscal Policy Regime Change and Third-Period Neutrality

| Time | TOTRES/GEXP | ABASE/TAXES | TOTRES/TRANSFER | FCHNG/GEXP | M1/GEXP |
|------|-------------|-------------|-----------------|------------|---------|
| t | 44.674 | 166.648 | 44.674 | 3.9 | 381.1 |
| t + 1 | 44.674 | 166.648 | 44.674 | 3.9 | 381.1 |
| t + 2 | 44.674 | 166.648 | 44.674 | 3.9 | 381.1 |
| t + 3 | 44.674 | 166.648 | 44.674 | 3.9 | 381.1 |
| t + 4 | 43.891 | 165.577 | 43.064 | 10.95 | 377.023 |
| t + 5 | 45.791 | 167.309 | 45.284 | 25.269 | 385.17 |
| t + 6 | 44.921 | 166.464 | 43.910 | 358.487 | 381.423 |
| t + 7 | 44.843 | 166.02 | 42.695 | 98.016 | 380.491 |
| t + 8 | 44.579 | 165.043 | 39.975 | − 7928.87 | 378.138 |
| t + 9 | 49.148 | 171.973 | 51.251 | − 7875.09 | 402.982 |
| t + 10 | 41.475 | 160.973 | 29.97 | 169176.0 | 362.54 |

Table VI.12. Time Paths for Accommodative Monetary Policy given Fiscal Policy Path as 3 Percent Growth and NAP 1

| Time | TOTRES/GEXP | ABASE/TAXES | TOTRES/TRANSFER | FCHNG/GEXP | M1/GEXP |
|---|---|---|---|---|---|
| t | 44.674 | 166.648 | 44.674 | 3.9 | 381.1 |
| t + 1 | 44.674 | 166.648 | 44.674 | 3.9 | 381.1 |
| t + 2 | 37.488 | 149.413 | 33.978 | − 0.861 | 361.165 |
| t + 3 | 44.622 | 163.486 | 41.648 | 6.679 | 380.807 |
| t + 4 | 49.354 | 163.838 | 43.461 | 17.113 | 375.322 |
| t + 5 | 59.818 | 168.812 | 48.02 | 40.264 | 376.728 |
| t + 6 | 27.904 | 126.124 | 18.844 | 19.608 | 329.139 |
| t + 7 | 104.572 | 211.079 | 70.905 | 138.769 | 446.406 |
| t + 8 | 73.138 | 140.881 | 34.294 | 182.336 | 314.953 |
| t + 9 | 92.94 | 155.81 | 38.017 | 321.926 | 365.888 |
| t + 10 | 67.33 | 125.062 | 15.254 | 484.487 | 328.656 |

Table VI.13. Time Paths for Accommodative Monetary Policy
given Fiscal Policy Path as 3 Percent Growth and NAP 3

| Time | TOTRES/GEXP | ABASE/TAXES | TOTRES/TRANSFER | FCHNG/GEXP | M1/GEXP |
|---|---|---|---|---|---|
| t | 44.674 | 166.648 | 44.674 | 3.9 | 381.1 |
| t + 1 | 44.674 | 166.648 | 44.674 | 3.9 | 381.1 |
| t + 2 | 44.674 | 166.648 | 44.674 | 3.9 | 381.1 |
| t + 3 | 44.674 | 166.648 | 44.674 | 3.9 | 381.1 |
| t + 4 | 18.438 | 125.991 | 17.425 | − 22.582 | 335.955 |
| t + 5 | 72.84 | 181.421 | 59.236 | 46.027 | 388.843 |
| t + 6 | 28.282 | 157.984 | 31.652 | − 23.686 | 401.148 |
| t + 7 | 26.806 | 137.733 | 25.334 | − 10.984 | 353.456 |
| t + 8 | 5.980 | 106.224 | 8.44 | − 29.191 | 302.523 |
| t + 9 | 208.877 | 288.028 | 121.687 | 253.474 | 582.508 |
| t + 10 | −217.163 | 16.412 | −75.602 | −435.707 | 273.394 |

periods for nap *j*, (e.g., change in monetary instrument is implemented after the first year for first-period neutrality but implemented after 3 years for nap 3). We use accommodative monetary policy to offset the fiscal policy effects under both first and third period neutrality. Since the initial effects of the fiscal policy measures seem to increase inequality (in particular, GEXP and TAXES) through the first few periods after the constant regime change, the program to offset those fiscal policy effects by monetary policy can require substantial changes in the monetary aggregate from year to year. As expected, time paths for the monetary policy variables show that some quite large (and politically unlikely) swings are necessary to achieve a fixed target level for the distribution parameter. The monetary policymaker faces the prospect of having to impose large changes in a monetary aggregate in order to offset relatively small changes in the fiscal policy. Clearly, the target inequality level can be achieved only at the cost of other macroeconomic objectives. It is unlikely that wide swings in a monetary variable will be consistent with any other reasonable macroeconomic goal.

## IX. CONCLUSION

This paper utilizes a model of income inequality to examine the dynamical adjustment path by which various fiscal and monetary policies work through the economy, to affect the size distribution of total income. Using a polynomial lag structures, we are able to specify how several distinct monetary (and fiscal) policy variables gradually change the distribution of income over time.

In the first part of the paper, we examine various fiscal/monetary policy combinations that are assumed to affect inequality based on a second order, four period distributed lag model. Fiscal policy, defined either as government expenditures or taxes, seem to first increase and then decrease inequality in conjunction with monetary policy variables. The effects of monetary policy seem to be biased towards reducing inequality. The result that transfers decrease inequality, is not surprising since they may be considered in part as redistributive instruments.

The results for monetary policies in conjunction with the fiscal policies varied depending on the monetary policy in question. For the adjusted monetary base, the level of total reserves and the nominal money supply, the results are consistent. In all three cases the effect appears to be towards less inequality. As noted in the text, the redistributional implications of inflation are not clear. For a change in the holding of securities by the Federal Reserve the results seem to be in the direction of increasing inequality. These results are contrary to those we found in a static model. In our earlier analysis we found that fiscal policy generally increases the inequality of total income, while monetary policy measures decrease the degree of inequality of total income. In our distributed lag model, these initial effects are repeated, however, allowing for policy effects to persist past the immediate impact, there is a trend to reverse the direction of change upon income inequality.

By looking at various policy combinations, we are able to show how the distribution parameter $c$, responds to proposed policy simulations. The long run effect of a given action is the net of results induced in successive periods. We expand this discussion to look at neutral policy actions. We ask how a policy variable must be manipulated to neutralize any exogenous impact on the level of inequality. We present some simulations to show what policies would have to be implemented to yield neutrality.

Finally, we present the actual time paths of various measures of neutrality to show that the time paths vary greatly depending on how one defines neutrality. Great caution must be taken when implementing policies which have the specific aim of neutral distributional effects. For example, when considering a policy action to (say) stimulate aggregate demand, the policymaker faces the problem that this will probably have an adverse effect on the income distribution. However, just by being aware that such a trade-off might occur, the policymaker is provided both timely and relevant information that should induce more efficacious decision-making.

## NOTES

1. See Friedman (1971), p. 27.
2. See Friedman (1968), p. 21.
3. See Modigliani and Ando (1976), p. 17.
4. Representative David R. Obey, chairman of the Joint Economic

Committee, charges: "The move to tax breaks for the rich that began with the arrival of the Reagan administration has almost certainly done nothing to narrow the gap between rich and poor since 1983." (*Wall Street Journal*, July 27, 1986).

5. The Joint Economic Committee report is from the *Wall Street Journal*, August 21, 1986.

6. Thurow (1970), Muellbauer (1974), Blinder and Esaki (1978) and Slottje (1987), among others, have looked at the redistribution implications of relative price changes.

7. Thus, the marginal distributions of each income component are hypothesized to be BII as is the marginal distribution of total income. If we attempted this relation with a lognormal distribution, it obviously wouldn't hold.

8. Basmann (1984a, 1984b), McDonald (1984) and Slottje (1984, 1987) have all discussed the merits of the Beta II distribution as an approximation to actual income data.

9. As noted above, the BII is only useful if it fits the data well. Slottje (1984, 1987) has shown that the BII provides a very good fit to the IRS data used in this study.

10. The variables are from the Economic Report of the President, 1985 and various issues of the *Treasury Bulletin*.

11. Tables for each policy measure combination are available from the authors upon request.

12. We also note that both our hypothetical distributions are approximated well by the Beta II distribution based upon the k-criterion, making our example meaningful, (cf. Kendall and Stuart, 1958).

13. Similarly, in the previous section the result may not be "pure" expenditure effects. The estimation bias arises due to an excluded variable.

14. With any positive value of each of our policy variables a constant growth rate implies an unbounded value as $t \to \infty$. If the bracketed term is non-zero then the change in income distribution parameter $c \to +\infty$ or $-\infty$, as the bracketed term is positive, or negative, respectively. Of course, this state of affairs commonly arises in models using linear specifications. For our five-year horizon the changes in $c$ are finite for any given point in time. If the bracketed term in (15) is positive (negative), $A_t \to \infty$, and the change in the distribution parameter will approach infinity (negative infinity).

15. The issue of the appropriate "intermediate" target for monetary policy, whether the target interest rates or reserve aggregates, has been addressed by Pesek and Saving (1967), Friedman (1971), and more recently Garcia (1984), among others.

# APPENDIX I

Define the beta distribution of the second kind as the joint distribution of the various income components which are representable by the joint distribution function

$$F_{y_1, \ldots, y_n}(y_1, \ldots, y_n)$$

$$= \int_{-\infty}^{y_n} \cdots \int_{-\infty}^{y_1} \frac{K^{b*} y_1^{c_1-1} \ldots, y_n^{c_n-1}}{B(c_1, \ldots, c_n; b*)[K + y]^{b*}} \, dy_1 \ldots dy_n$$

$$y = y_1 + y_2 + \ldots + y_n \qquad\qquad y_j > 0$$
$$b*, c_j > 0$$

(where $y_j$ represents the $j$th income component and $k$ is the lower terminal of the joint distribution. $b*$ is called the Pareto parameter because, under certain conditions on $b*$, the distribution becomes a Pareto distribution. The $c$'s are called inequality parameters for reasons demonstrated below. Inequality in any component can be analyzed simply by integrating out everything else. From the joint distribution function (A.1), the marginal density function of income component $j$ takes the form,

$$f(y) = \frac{K^{b*} y_j^{c_j-1}}{B(c_j, b*)[K + y])^{b*+c_j}} \tag{A.2}$$

Again, recall the special property of the Beta distribution of the second kind that the sum of the marginals of the various components maintain the same form as the marginal distribution of total income. Thus, the marginal distribution of total income take the form,

$$f(y) = \frac{K^{b*} y^{c-1}}{B(c, b*)[K + y])^{b*+c}} \tag{A.3}$$

where

$$c = c_1 + c_2 + \ldots + c_{10} \tag{A.4}$$

Equations (A.2) and (A.3) provide the necessary framework to study inequality between income components and total income.

From the marginal distribution of total income given in (A.3), the first moment is

$$\mu_1' = kc/(b* - 1), \qquad (A.5)$$

the second moment is

$$\mu_2' = \frac{k^2 \Gamma(c + 2)\Gamma(b* - 2)\Gamma(b* + c)}{\Gamma(b* + c)\Gamma(c)\Gamma(b*)} = \frac{k^2 c(c + 1)}{(b* - 2)(b* - 1)} \qquad (A.6)$$

and the variance is

$$s^2 = \mu_2' - (\mu_1')^2 = \frac{k?_1'(c + 1)}{(b* - 2)(b* - 1)} = \frac{\mu_1'(\mu_1' + k)}{(b* - 2)}, \qquad (A.7)$$

*Table A.1.* Some Hypothetical Income Distributions and Associated Summary Statistics

| $F_{y_a}$ | $F_{y_b}$ |
|---|---|
| 2000 | 4000 |
| 2500 | 5000 |
| 260 | 5200 |
| 3200 | 6400 |
| 4000 | 7575 |
| 4500 | 8000 |
| 5000 | 8080 |
| 5500 | 8585 |
| 5600 | 8686 |
| 6200 | 9000 |
| 7500 | 9595 |
| 8000 | 9595 |
| 8500 | 10000 |
| 8600 | 10100 |
| 9500 | 10100 |
| 9500 | 11000 |
| 10000 | 11200 |
| 10000 | 12200 |
| 12000 | 12400 |
| 13200 | 13332 |
| 14000 | 14140 |
| 15500 | 15655 |
| 15500 | 15655 |

Table A.1. (Continued)

| $^F y_a$ | $^F y_b$ |
|---|---|
| 16000 | 16160 |
| 16200 | 16362 |
| 17000 | 17170 |
| 17500 | 17675 |
| 17600 | 17776 |
| 18200 | 18382 |
| 18600 | 18786 |
| 19500 | 20475 |
| 20000 | 21000 |
| 20000 | 21000 |
| 20000 | 21000 |
| 21000 | 22050 |
| 21500 | 22575 |
| 22000 | 23100 |
| 25000 | 26250 |
| 27000 | 28350 |
| 29000 | 30450 |
| 31000 | 31000 |
| 32000 | 32000 |
| 33000 | 33000 |
| 35000 | 35000 |
| 42000 | 42000 |
| 45000 | 45000 |
| 50000 | 50000 |
| 100000 | 100000 |
| 250000 | 250000 |
| 1000000 | 944941 |

| | | |
|---|---|---|
| Mean income: | $42940 | $42940 |
| Variance: | 20407943265 | 18246422175 |
| $b^*$: | 2.0982 | 2.10984 |
| $c$: | 12.6498 | 12.7838 |
| Gini Coefficient: | 0.502123 | 0.500038 |

$^F y_a$ is the initial income distribution.
$^F y_b$ is the income distribution after transfer action.

# Chapter VII

# *Policy Responses to Inequality*

## I. INTRODUCTION

The evidence presented in Chapter V suggests that the size distribution of current income is contemporaneously affected by changes in fiscal and monetary policy. In Chapter VI, a distributed-lag version was adopted so that we could detect policy effects on the distribution of current income through time, as well as the contemporaneous effect observed in the previous chapter. The results from the distributed-lag models indicate that changes in lagged values of the policy variables do appear to be significant in explaining changes in the level of inequality. In other words, changes in policy tend to precede changes in the level of inequality. Thus, the results from the distributed-lag models are consistent with changes in fiscal and monetary policy "causing" changes in inequality.[1,2] Although capable of inducing changes in the size distribution of income, the results from previous chapter do not indicate whether government policy actions are sensitive to changes in the level of inequality. Or, do increases in the level of inequality cause the government to initiate actions to redistribute income?

The idea that policymakers are sensitive to increases in the level of inequality reflects a strong belief that the government can affect the size distribution of income. In other words, a necessary condition for the government to engage in redistributive efforts is that the available policy tools can indeed redistribute income. Evidence supporting this proposition is found in Chapters V and VI, as well as in studies by Musgrave, Case, and Leonard (1974) and Pechman and Okner (1974).[3] Without either theoretical or empirical support that the necessary condition is satisfied, one could not justify giving charge over income redistribution to the government.

The evidence suggests that monetary and fiscal policy does affect the size distribution of income. However, does the government consciously use policy variables to reshape the distribution? That is, is income redistribution a decision variable for the government? Or, are the observed effects of fiscal and monetary policy merely by-products of government attempting to achieve other goals?

Recall in Chapter II that income redistribution was not one of the ultimate goals listed in the Employment Act of 1946. Despite the absence of income equality from that list, casual observation of politics in the United States suggests that maintaining some degree of equality in the distribution of current income is desirable. Perhaps the clearest examples of the importance of income redistribution are the "New Frontier" and "Great Society" programs initiated during the Kennedy and Johnson administrations. Largely, these policies were directed at reshaping the distribution by raising living standards of those in the low-income groups.

The purpose of this chapter is to investigate the possible causal relationships between monetary and fiscal policy variables and the level of inequality. Our earlier results suggest that changes in policy do "cause" changes in the level of inequality. Therefore, the primary insight we hope to gain from this investigation is whether policymakers respond to changes in the size distribution of income. To detect the causal orderings we will use innovations in the economic time-series in a cross-correlation function. The estimated coefficients of the cross-correlation function will indicate whether changes in policy variables tend to precede changes in the level of inequality, or changes in inequality lead changes in policy variables, or both.[4]

In Section II we will consider several theories explaining why the government would be interested in redistributive efforts. Section III will discuss the methodology employed to detect the causal relationships. Section VI will present the results of our causality test and conclude this book.

## II. THE GOVERNMENT'S INTEREST IN REDISTRIBUTIVE EFFORTS

It is generally accepted that the government has a role in achieving goals in the broad areas of price stability, unemployment, output growth and income redistribution. The relative importance of each of these goals, however, is not well defined. In fact, it is likely that preferences toward income distribution relative to output growth change through time.

To illustrate how changing preferences might influence the observed "total" effect of a change in the level of inequality it may be useful to decompose the total effect into a "preference" effect and a "direct" effect. The former effect captures the weight given by policymakers to income redistribution relative to other goals. For instance, an increase in the weight would mean greater emphasis given to income redistribution as opposed to, price stability. The latter reflects the response of policy to a change in inequality, with income redistribution as the only goal.

Consider the case where the preference effect is equal to zero. If we think of preference effect as a weight applied to the direct effect, such that the total effect is the product of these two components, it is unlikely that redistributive efforts would be sensitive to changes in the level of inequality. The total effect equal to zero would reflect the absence of value given to income redistribution by policymakers.

Of course, a preference effect equal to zero is a special case. In general, the government will give some positive weight to income redistribution as a policy goal. Several reasons have been given in the literature explaining the importance of maintaining some degree of income equality. For our purposes, these reasons also serve as the basis for explaining why inequality may cause policy.

One reason given to explain why the government should be concerned about the distribution of current income is that households' value income redistribution. Petersen (1967) argued a "major cause of the expanded role of the economy's public sector has been the emergence and increasing public acceptance of the concept of the welfare state."[5] Petersen suggests that the public sanctioned the federal government to become more active in its role in maintaining a minimum standard of living for society's members.

To explain the private sector's added emphasis on the importance of other's welfare, Hochman and Rodgers (1969) formalized a theory that an individual's utility is "interdependent." That is, one individual's utility level depends on the utility of other members of the population. The upshot is that the federal government took a more active role in response to the private sector's mandate.

Although households may value income, this does not explain why the government chooses more or less redistributive efforts. One explanation linking household and government behavior assumes that policymakers maximize a social welfare function.[6] In its simplest specification, social welfare is simply the sum of each individual's utility level. Therefore, the government acts as an extension of the private sector. Supposition of this optimizing behavior by the government suggests that a necessary condition for income redistribution to be an argument in the government's maximizing problem is that redistribution appears in the (representative) individual's utility function. This follows from the implicit specification of the government as a passive agent whose behavior reflects decisions actually made at the household level.

An alternative explanation for a position that a government values income redistribution rests on a quite different view of the government's objective function. Basing policymaker's decision upon interdependent utility functions means that government is acting as an agent, simply carrying out (perhaps more efficiently) the public's wishes. Another view of the government maintains that individuals who exercise governmental authority make decisions that maximize the likelihood of staying in power.[7] Thus, contrary to conducting passively the policies chosen to further goals by society, this objective function suggests that policymakers are active by selecting policies to further their own objectives and goals. The time paths of the policy variables would then reflect maximizing behavior of policymakers as opposed to maximizing behavior of society.

Policymakers receive rents not available to the general electorate. Consequently, the specification of the objective function reflects this desire. It must be recognized that income redistribution policies may simply reflect policymakers wish to stay in power.

Clearly, increases in inequality may have adverse repercussions for policymakers. Myrdal (1968) postulated that if inequality attained critical mass, those in the low-income groups would react with the intention of replacing the current ruling regime. Observing huge disparity in the distribution of current income may induce individuals in low-income groups to form coalitions. Through coalitions, which may contain a large percentage of the population, these groups can overthrow a government. To the extent that policymakers consider avoiding potentially adverse political ramifications of increasing inequality, income redistribution is a likely candidate for inclusion in a government objective function. For instance, an increase in the level of inequality is likely to elicit a government response. To minimize potentially damaging effects of rising inequality, policymakers are inclined to implement monetary and fiscal policy changes which may lead to a more equitable distribution of current income.

Consider the case where inequality decreases. Policymakers' desire to stay in power can conceivably result in either a more or less active role in income redistribution. With a decline in the level of inequality, the political repercussions envisioned by Myrdal are likely to be given less consideration because the movement in the distribution of current income is favorable to policymakers. Consequently, the government may respond with a more restrictive stance toward inequality. It is also possible that the government would respond to more equality in the distribution of current income with more active policy toward income redistribution. Policymakers may wish to "invest" in redistributive activities thereby signaling the importance of this goal to the electorate. Moreover, if the policy actions involved that achieve more equality also achieve, higher output growth, there may be added incentive to engage in more redistribution. While government responses to changes in the level of inequality may be consistent regardless of the motive for income redistribution being in the objective function, it is possible that policymakers may consider a broader set of actions when maximizing "self-serving" objective function compared to policies considered when optimizing with respect to a social welfare function.

## III. RESULTS OF "CAUSALITY" TESTS

Several approaches have been developed to detect causal relationships between economic time series. Most notable, perhaps, are the methodologies presented by Granger (1969), Sims (1972) and Pierce and Haugh (1979). In this analysis we will adopt the Pierce-Haugh procedure which uses the cross-correlation function to uncover temporal precedence.

The Pierce-Haugh approach is bivariate analysis which identifies temporal precedence using a two-step procedure. The first step involves use of Box-Jenkins univariate techniques to decompose stationary time-series into its deterministic and innovations series.[8] In the second step, we calculate the cross-correlation function using the innovations derived in the first step. Formally, the cross-correlation function is expressed as follows:

$$\rho(k) = \Sigma u_{t-k} \, V_t \, / \, [\Sigma(u_t)^2 \, (V_t)^2]^{1/2} \tag{7.1}$$

where $u$ and $v$ denote innovations obtained from two distinct time-series using the univariate techniques described in the first step of the procedure.

Table VII.1 lists the four basic causal relationships which may be identified using the Pierce-Haugh approach. Detection of temporal precedence uses values of the cross-correlation function. If, for instance, values of the cross-correlation are statistically insignificant, we infer that the two time-series in question are independent. If, however, $\rho(k)$ is significantly different from zero for some positive value of $k$, $u$ is said to "cause" $v$.[9] More accurately, the changes in the time-series associated with innovations denoted $u$ tends to temporally precede changes in the series associated with the series denoted $v$. Conversely, if $\rho(k)$ is significantly different from zero for some negative values of $k$, $v$ causes $u$. Finally, if statistical significance is found for $k > 0$ *and* $k < 0$, causality is said to be bidirectional.

One drawback to the Pierce-Haugh approach for causality test-

*Table VII.I.* Basic Causal Relationships Indicated
By Cross-correlation Coefficients

| *Value of Cross-correlation Coefficient* | *Causal Relationship* |
|---|---|
| $\rho_k = 0$ all k | u is independent of v |
| $\rho_k \neq 0$ some k > 0 | u "causes" v |
| $\rho_k \neq 0$ some k < 0 | v "causes" u |
| $\rho_k \neq 0$ some k > 0 *and* some k < 0 | u "causes" v *and* "causes" u (bi-directional causality) |

ing is that it is limited to pairwise analysis between series. In our context, however, it is possible that relationships between fiscal and monetary policy variables (e.g., the government budget constraint) may complicate detection of "true causal" relationships. Consider the coordination scheme postulated by Sargent and Wallace (1981) where actions of the monetary authority are constrained by independently-set fiscal policy. With fiscal policy dominating monetary policy, the monetary authority must finance "any discrepancy between the revenue demanded by the fiscal authority and the amount of bonds that can be sold to the public." In this case, innovations in a fiscal policy variable are likely to be coincident with innovations in monetary policy variables. In a bivariate setting, no partial effect of a change in monetary policy, given fiscal policy, is observable. We can take some solace from the fact that our earlier model specifications did capture partial effects of both fiscal and monetary policy. Unfortunately, these models did not examine the possibility of feedback from changes in the parameter of the size distribution of income to changes in the policy variables.

Although the distribution parameter was found to be stationary, each of the policy variables required some transformation to achieve stationarity in their respective mean and variance. The necessary transformations, as well as the univariate models used to decompose the time-series into its deterministic and innovation parts are recorded. The policy variables used in this analysis are government expenditures, transfer payments, the market value of publicly-held government debt, the adjusted monetary base, total reserves and the change in the Federal Reserve's holdings of Treasury securities.

The results of the cross-correlation analysis applied to innovations of each policy variable combined with the innovations in the distribution parameter are reported in Charts VII.1–VII.7. In general, we then observe results from the cross-correlation analysis that are consistent with the relationships indicated in the regression models presented in earlier chapters. In other words, the causality as suggested by statistically significant cross-correlation coefficients appears to run unidirectionally from the policy variables to the distribution parameter. With ABASE, however, the results indicate that causality runs from inequality to policy and not the other direction.

In three cases, however, the cross-correlation coefficient is statis-

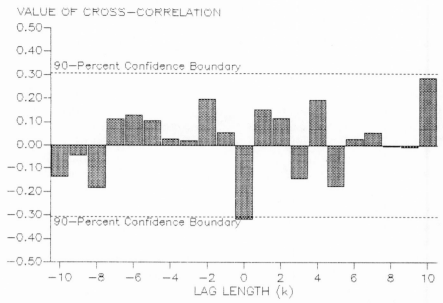

*Chart VII.1.* Cross-correlations between Government Expenditures and Total Income Distribution Parameter.

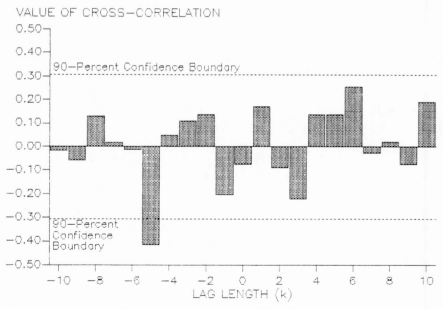

*Chart VII.2.* Cross-correlations between Adjusted Monetary Base and Total Income Distribution Parameter.

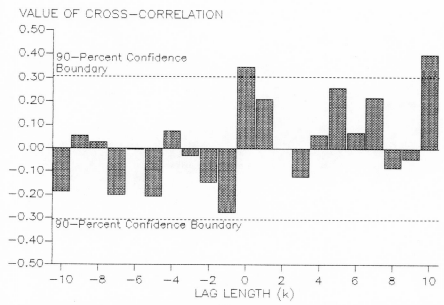

*Chart VII.3.* Cross-correlations between M1 and Total Income Distribution Parameter.

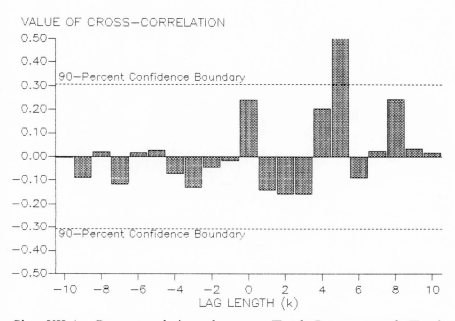

*Chart VII.4.* Cross-correlations between Total Reserves and Total Income Distribution Parameter.

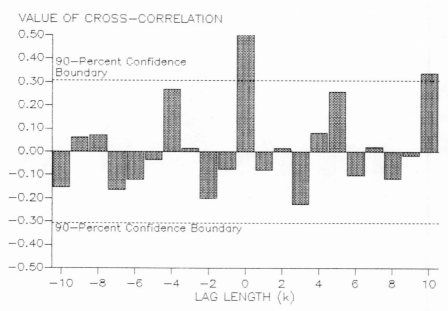

*Chart VII.5.* Cross-correlations between Transfer Payments and Total Income Distribution Parameter.

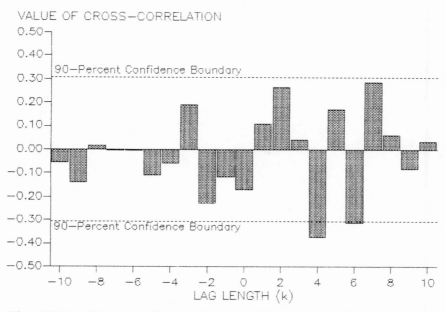

*Chart VII.6.* Cross-correlations between Changes in Fed's Holdings of Treasury Securities and Total Income Distribution Parameter.

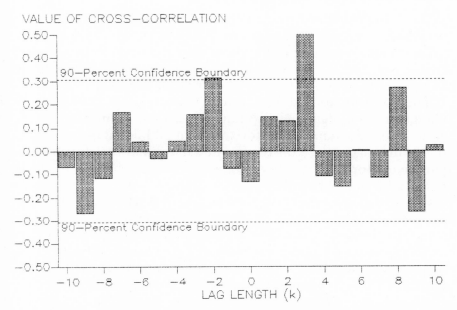

VALUE OF CROSS—CORRELATION

*Chart VII.7.* Cross-correlations between Market Value of Publicly-held Government Debt and Total Income Distribution Parameter.

tically significant only when $k = 0$. With GEXP, M1 and TRANS-FER as the policy measures, the presence of a significant cross-correlation at $k = 0$ indicates instantaneous causality.

With a statistically significant cross-correlation coefficient at $k = 0$, either of two unidirectional relationships are suggested. For instance, it is easy to imagine that an increase in transfer payments would affect the size distribution of current income within the current period. With the time unit of measurement being one year, it is plausible that changes in government expenditures or the money supply could induce changes in the level of inequality, as well. Therefore, one relationship which is consistent with the data is that changes in policy temporally precede changes in inequality. In other words, policy causes inequality.

Consider an exogenous increase in unemployment. The swelling ranks of the unemployed means lower economic activity is likely and a reshaping of the distribution of income toward more inequality. In response to the rising unemployment level, the government is likely to engage in more stimulative policy. In this case, changes in the level of inequality temporally precede changes in policy. This case is consistent with the result obtained in the cross-correlation analysis. Consequently, the data support both cases of unidirectional causality with a significant cross-correlation coefficient at $k = 0$. As Pierce and Haugh note, it is impossible to ascertain the direction of causality from the data.

The downside to finding instantaneous causality, as Pierce and Haugh note, is that the direction of causality cannot be ascertained from the data. Therefore, without additional information, these three cases are consistent with changes in the distribution parameter for total income helping to predict changes in fiscal policy and monetary policy, or vice-versa.

Contrary to the other policy measures, with ABASE as the measure of the monetary policy, it appears that unidirectional causality runs from inequality to policy. As indicated in the chart, the value of the cross-correlation coefficient at $k = -2$ is significant. The negative sign of the cross-correlation coefficient suggests that a rise in the distribution parameter tends to precede a decline in the rate of growth in the adjusted monetary base. Recall that the partial derivative of the Gini coefficient with respect to a change in the distribution parameter, $c$, is negative. Since a decrease (increase) in the Gini coefficient ($c$) indicates that the distribution of current income is more equal, the cross-correlation coefficient suggests that a more equitable distribution tends to precede more restrictive monetary policy.

Bidirectional causality is indicated in only one case. With the market value of publicly-held government debt as the fiscal policy measure, Table VII.7 shows that statistically significant cross-correlation coefficients occur at both positive and negative values of $k$. The results are consistent with changes in fiscal policy helping to predict changes in the level of inequality *and* changes in inequality helping to predict changes in fiscal policy. The signs of the significant cross-correlation coefficients are somewhat puzzling. On the one hand, the coefficient at $k = 3$ suggests that an increase in the federal deficit leads to current income being distributed more equally. Or, stimulative fiscal policy causes inequality to fall. The results suggest that stimulative fiscal policy does "trickle down" to disproportionately help those in low-income groups.

On the other hand, a significant coefficient at $k < 0$ is also present in Chart VII.7 and its value is positive. This result is consistent with a decrease in the level of inequality causing fiscal policy to be more stimulative. Conversely, when the level of inequality rises, more restrictive fiscal policy follows. In our discussion of motives for policymakers to respond to changes in the level of inequality, we argued that more inequality would expectedly give rise to policy actions designed to subsequently lower inequality. Yet, these results indicate that the government responds to increase in inequality with fiscal policy which apparently induces subsequent greater inequality.

What can we infer about the alternative motives for including income redistribution in the government objective function based on the results? There are only cases where the results unambiguously support inequality causing policy. In our discussion motivating policymaker concern for income redistribution we noted usual specifications of a social welfare function explain an inverse relationship between changes in inequality and changes in policy. That is, an increase in policy would tend to precede policies which lower inequality. Certainly, the results obtained with ABASE as the monetary policy measure are consistent with this explanation.

Alternatively, motivation for including income redistribution may reflect policymakers' desire to stay in power. It was argued that a self-serving policymaker may exhibit either a positive or negative relationship to changes in inequality. Consequently, the results using ABASE as the monetary policy measure and the market value of publicly-held government debt as the fiscal policy measure are consistent with policymakers maximizing their own utility functions. Thus, the causal relationship between government debt and inequality (tentatively) supports the hypothesis that the fiscal authority maximize a self-serving objective function, whereas evidence about the monetary authority is inconclusive between the alternative motives.

## IV. SUMMARY

In this chapter we examined the issue of causality between policy and the level of inequality in the size distribution of current income. Since much of the earlier text provided simple explanations relating possible channels through which changes in policy may affect the level of inequality, we offered a brief description of how more or less equality may induce changes in policy behavior. To detect causality, we adopted the two-step approach suggested by Pierce and Haugh.

In general, the results coming from the cross-correlation analysis are consistent with the earlier results which indicated that policy causes inequality. The results using four measures of monetary and fiscal policy should be discussed separately. Three of the four cases exhibit instantaneous causality. With M1 as the monetary policy measure, or with GEXP or TRANSFERS as the fiscal policy measures, the data support any of the following three causal relationships: policy causes inequality, inequality causes policy, or both. Certainly, this result is consistent with our finding that changes in policy variables tend to precede changes in the level of inequality. Unfortunately, it is not possible if this is the "true" state of affairs using this approach.

In one case, the results clearly go against the idea that policy causes inequality. With ABASE as the monetary policy measure, the results indicate that changes in inequality tend to precede changes in monetary policy. Since using TOTRES as the monetary policy measure gives a contradictory result, this is hardly conclusive evidence that monetary policy is sensitive to the level of inequality.

Bidirectional causality is indicated with the market value of publicly-held government debt as the fiscal policy measure. The cross-correlation function indicates that increases in debt outstanding gives rise to a more equal distribution of current income and increases in inequality induce more restrictive fiscal policy by policymakers. This result contradicts our expectation of government response to greater inequality with policies designed to lessen inequality. In the context of a reduction in inequality, it is possible, however, that the fiscal authority would increase redistribution efforts so as to signal his intention toward inequality. The signal serves as an investment on the part of the policymaker to increase the likelihood that he stays in power.

Finally, we urge the reader to consider the results presented here as preliminary. The conclusions must be viewed as very tentative given the few observations available. Nonetheless, the results do suggest the possibility of a bidirectional relationship between policy and inequality, which may be ferreted out more clearly in the future. Balke and Slottje (1989) and Haslag and

Slottje (1989) have begun a rigorous examination of these issues. In addition, the preliminary results reported here are interesting from the perspective of policymakers' objective functions. A line of future may be to further delve into policymakers' motives for including income redistribution in their optimization problem.

The purpose of this book has been to make the reader aware that monetary (as well as fiscal) policy may have substantial re-distributive effects. To the extent that equality in the distribution of income is a policy goal, the preliminary evidence presented here suggests that the monetary authority should integrate policy effects on the level of inequality into his decision-making process when contemplating alternative policy actions.

## NOTES

1. In the literature, *causality* is used very tentatively. Although pregnant with meaning, economists appear to have settled on a narrow interpretation that the word *cause* is roughly equivalent to detecting temporal precedence. In other words, if government expenditures causes changes in the of inequality, it is more accurate to state changes in government expenditures help to predict changes in the level of inequality. For brevity, the word cause is often substituted with the above meaning.

2. The earlier analyses was carried out with data that was nonstationary in the mean and variance. Because "levels" were used in the regressions, it is possible that spurious correlation was detected. Moreover, lagged values of the dependent variable were not used as is the typical case in causality analysis. Therefore, one must qualify earlier findings reported here as being consistent with policy causing inequality.

3. In both of the studies cited here, only the effects of fiscal policy were analyzed. The underlying assumption being that monetary policy does not influence the level of inequality.

4. As Pierce and Haugh note, two-sided relations between innovations of economic time-series are analogous to similar relations between the stationary series themselves.

5. See Petersen, p. 239.

6. See Rosen (1988) for a more complete description and analysis of a government maximizing a social welfare function.

7. Examples of this type of government maximizing behavior may be found in Barro and Gordon (1983) and Cukierman and Meltzer (1986).

8. Innovations are obtained from stationary time-series using univariate Box-Jenkins techniques. That part that is not explained by the

past history (where the appropriate history is suggested by the Box-Jenkins analysis, is referred to as "innovations." Stationarity is checked formally using the Dickey-Fuller test statistic. On an informal basis, we note that a plot of the original (i.e., untransformed) series suggested nonstationarity in the mean and variance for each of the policy variables which tended to dampen very slowly. Following some simple transformations, such as first differencing or differencing the logs, stationarity was achieved as indicated by a plot of the transformed data and quickly dampening autocorrelation functions. Finally, the Box-Ljung Q-statistic indicated that the residuals were consistent with the supposition of "white noise" for the models reported in Table VII.2.

9.   The cross-correlation coefficient is asymptotically distributed as an independent normal with a mean of zero and a variance of $1/n$ (see Ashley, Granger and Schmalensee (1980) for a more detailed exposition).

# References

Aitchison, J. and J. A. C. Brown (1969). The Lognormal Distribution with *Special Reference to Its Uses in Economics*. Cambridge: Cambridge University Press.

Almon, S. (1965). "The Distributed Lag Between Capital Appropriations and Expenditures," *Econometrica* 33, 178–196.

Ashley, R., C. W. J. Granger and R. Schmalensee (1980). "Advertising and Aggregate Consumption: An Analysis of Causality," *Econometrica,* 48, 1149–67.

Atkinson, A. B. (1970). "On the Measurement of Inequality," *Journal of Economic Theory* 2, 244–263.

Atkinson, A. B. and F. Bourguignon (1982). The comparion of multidimensioned distributions of economic status. *Review of Economic Studies,* 49, 183–201.

Bach, R. L. and Ando, A. (1957). "The Redistributional Effects of Inflation," *Review of Economic Statistics* 39, 1–13.

Balke, N. and D. J. Slottje (1989). "A macroeconomic Model of Income Inequality," Working paper #8902, Dallas Texas.

Barro, R. J. and D. B. Gordon (1983). "Rules, Discretion and Reputation on a Model of Monetary Policy," *Journal of Monetary Economics,* 12, 101–22.

Basmann, R. L., D. J. Molina and D. J. Slottje (1984). "Variable Preference, Economic Inequality and the Cost of Living Index," *Advances in Econometrics* 3, 1–69.

Basmann, R. L., D. J. Molina, M. Rodarte, and D. J. Slottje (1984). "Some New Methods of Predicting Changes in Economic Inequality Associated with Trends in Growth and Development," in *Issues in Third World Development,* K. Nobe and R. K. Sampath (eds.), Denver: Westview Press.

Basmann, R. L., and D. J. Slottje (1987). "A New Index of Income Inequality: The B Measure," *Economic Letters* 24, 385–389.

Becker, Gary S. (1962). Investment in human capital: a theoretical analysis. *Journal of Political Economy,* 70, 9–49.

Becker, Gary S. (1967). *Human Capital and the Personal Distribution of Income: An Analytical Approach,* Woytinsky Lecture No. 1. Ann Arbor: University of Michigan, Institute of Public Administration.

Belsey, D. A., E. Kuh and R. E. Welch (1980). *Regression Diagnostics: I Identifying Influential Data and Sources of Collinearity,* Wiley, New York.

Blackorby, C., D. Donaldson, and M. Auersperg (1980). "A New Procedure for the Measurement of Inequality Within and Among Population Subgroups," discussion Paper 80-25, University of British Columbia, *Canadian Journal of Economics* 14, 665–685.

Blinder, A. and G. Esaki (1978). Macroeconomic Activity and Income and Distribution in the Post War U.S., *Review of Economic Statistics* 60, 604–608.

Bowles, S. (1969). *Planning Educational Systems for Economic Growth.* Harvard Economic Studies, vol. 133, Cambridge, Mass.: Harvard University Press.

Bronfenbenner, M. and Holzman, F. D. (1963). "Survey of Inflation Theory," *American Economic Review* 53, 593–661.

Buse, A. (1973). "Goodness of Fit in Generalized Least Squares Estimation," *The American Statistician* 27, 106–108.

Champernowne, D. G. (1952). "The Graduation of Income Distribution," *Econometrica* 20, 318–351.

Champernowne, D. G. (1974). "A Comparison of Measures of Inequality of Income Distribution," *Economic Journal* 84, 787–816.

Chiswick, B. R. (1974). *Income Inequality: Regional Analysis Within a Human Capital Framework.* New York: National Bureau of Economic Research, Columbia University Press.

Cowell, F. A. (1980). "On the Structure of Additive Inequality Measures," *Review of Economic Studies* 47, 521–531.

Cowell, F. (1977). *Measuring Inequality.* London: Phillip Allan.

Creedy, J. (1985). *Dynamics of Income Distribution,* London: B. Blackwell, Inc.

Cukierman, A. and A. H. Meltzer (1986). "A Theory of Ambiguity, Credibility and Inflation under Discretion and Asymmetric Information," *Econometrica* 54, 1099–1128.

Danziger, S., R. Haveman and R. Plotnick (1981). "How Income Transfers Affect Work, Savings and the Income Distribution: A Critical Review," *Journal of Economic Literature* 19, 975–1028.

Dougherty, C. R. S. (1971). Estimates of labour aggregate functions.

*Harvard Center for International Affairs, Economic Development Report,* No. 190, Cambridge: Development Research Group.

Dougherty, C. R. S. (1972). Substitution and the structure of the labour force. *Economic Journal,* 82, 170–182.

Durbin, J. and G. S. Watson (1950). "Testing for Serial Correlation Least-Squares Regression, I," *Biometrica* 37, 409–428.

Eltato, and E. Frigyes (1968). "New Income Inequality Measures," *Econometrica* 36, 383–392.

Elderton, W. P. (1938). *Frequency Curves and Correlation,* Cambridge: Cambridge University Press.

Fei, J. C. H., G. Ranis, and S. W. Y. Kuo (1978). "Growth and the Family Distribution of Income by Factor Components," *Quarterly Journal of Economics* 92, 17–53.

Fisher, F. M. (1956). "Income Distribution, Value Judgements and Welfare," *Econometrica* 29, 171–185.

Fisher, R. A. (1922). "On the Mathematical Foundation of Theoretical Statistics," *Phil. Trans. Roy. Soc. London,* Series A. 222.

Fisk, P. R. (1961). The graduation of income distributions. *Econometrica,* 29, 171–185.

Friedman, Milton (1953). Choice, chance, and the personal distribution of income. *Journal of Political Economy,* 61, 277–290.

Friedman, Milton (1975). *An Economist's Protest.* Glen Ridge, N.J.: Horton and Daughter's Publishing.

Fomby, T., R. C. Hill and S. R. Johnson (1984). *Advanced Econometric Methods,* New York: Springer-Verlag.

Foster, James (1983). "An Axiomatic Characterization of the Theil Measure of Income Inequality," *Journal of Economic Theory* 31, 105–121.

Friedman, M. (1968). "The Role of Monetary Policy," *American Economic Review* 58, 1–17.

Friedman, M. (1971). "A Monetary Theory of Nominal Income," *Journal of Political Economy* 79, 323–337.

Garcia, G. G. (1984). "The Right Rabbit: Which Intermediate Target Should the Fed Pursue?" *Economic Perspectives Federal Reserve Bank of Chicago,* 15–30.

Gini, C. (1912). *Variabilita e Mutabilita.* Bologna.

Gordon, R. J. (1981). *Macroeconomics,* New York: McGraw-Hill.

Granger, C. W. J. (1969). "Investigating Causal Relations by Econometric Models and Cross-spectral Methods," *Econometrica* 37, 424–38.

Gujarati, D. (1978). *Basic Econometrics,* New York: McGraw-Hill.

Haslag, J. and D. J. Slottje (1989). "An Error Correction Representation of Income Inequality," working paper #8923, SMU, Texas.

Hockman, H. M. and J. D. Rodgers (1969) "Pareto optimal Redistribution" AER 59, 542–557.

Hunt, J. M. (1961). *Intelligence and Experience.* New York: Ronald Press.

Jorgenson, D. W. and Dan Slesnick (1984). "Inequality in the Distribution of Individual Welfare," *Advances in Econometrics.*

Kadiyala, D. R. (1968). "A Transformation Used to Circumvent the Problem of Autocorrelation," *Econometrica* 36, 93–96.

Kakwani, N. (1980). "On a Class of Poverty Measures," *Econometrica* 48, 437–446.

Kendall, M. G. and Stuart, A. (1958). *The Advanced Theory of Statistics,* London: Charles W. Griffin.

Kessel, R. A. and Alchian, A. A. (1960). "The Inflation-Induced Lag of Wages," *American Economic Review* 50, 43–46.

King, M. A. (1983). "An Index of Inequality: With Applications t Horizontal Equity and Social Mobility," *Econometrica* 51, 99–115.

Kolm, S. (1977). "Multi-dimensional Egalitarianism," *Quarterly Journal of Economics* 91, 1–13.

Kuga, K. (1979). "Comparison of Inequality Measures: A Monte Carlo Study," *Economic Studies Quarterly* 30, 221–226.

Lorenz, M. D. (1905). Methods of measuring the concentration of wealth. *Journal of The American Statistical Association,* 9, 209–219.

Lydall, H. (1968). *The Structure of Labor Earnings.* Oxford: Oxford University Press.

Lydall, H. (1979). *A Theory of Income Distribution,* Oxford: Clarendon Press.

Maasoumi, Esfandiar (1986). The measurement and decomposition of multidimensional equality. *Econometrica,* 48, 1791–1803.

Maasoumi, E. (1984). "The Measurement and Decomposition of Multi-Dimensional Inequality," Indiana University, Department of Economics, Bloomington.

McDonald, J. B. and M. Ransom (1979). "Functional Forms, Estimation Techniques and the Distribution of Income," *Econometrica* 47, 1513–1516.

McDonald, J. B. (1984). "Some Generalized Functions for the Size Distribution of Income," *Econometrica* 52, 647–665.

Mincer, Jacob (1970). Investment in human capital and personal income ditribution. *Journal of Political Economy,* 66, 281–302.

Mincer, Jacob (1974). *Schooling, Experience and Earnings.* New York: National Bureau of Economic Research.

Modigliani, F. and Ando, A. (1976). "Impacts of Fiscal Actions on Aggregate Income and the Monetarist Controversy: Theory and Evidence," in J. L. Stein (ed.) *Monetarism,* New York: American Elsevier.

Morgan, J. (1962). "The Anatomy of Income Distribution," *Review of Economic Statistics* 44, 117–130.

Muellbauer, J. (1974). "Prices and Inequality: The United Kingdom Experience," *The Economic Journal* 84, 32–55.

Myrdal, G. (1968). *Asian Drama: An Inquiry into the Poverty of Nations*, vol. 2, New York: Twentieth Century Fund and Random House, Pantheon Books.

Ott, Lynn (1977). *An Introduction to Statistical Methods and Data Analysis*, New York: Duxbury Press.

Pareto, V. (1897). *Mauvale di Economica Politica*, Milan: Societa Editrice Libraria.

Parks, R. W. (1978). "Inflation and Relative Price Variability," *Journal of Political Economy* 86, 79–95.

Pechman, J. A. and B. J. Okner (1974). *Who Bears the Tax Burden?* Washington, D.C.: Brookings Institution.

Pesek, B. P. and Saving, T. R. (1967). *Money, Wealth and Economic Theory*, New York: Macmillan.

Peterson, Wallace C. (1967). *Income, Employment and Economic Growth*, W. W. Norton Co. New York.

Pierce, D. A. and L. D. Haugh (1979). "Causality in Temporal Systems: Characterizations and a Survey," *Journal of Econometrics* 5, 265–93.

Pigou, Arthur C. (1932). *The Economics of Welfare*, 4th edition. London: Macmillan.

Porter, P. K. and D. J. Slottje (1985). A Comprehensive Analysis of Inequality in the Size Distribution of Income for the United States 1952–1981, *Southern Economic Journal* 52, 412–422.

Psacharopoulos, G. and K. Hinchliffe (1972). Further evidence on the elasticity of substitution among different types of educated labor. *Journal of Political Economy*, 80, 786–796.

Rosen, Harvery S. (1988). *Public Finance* 2nd Edition Irwin; Homewood Il.

Russell, William, D. J. Slottje and J. H. Haslag (1986). "A Sensitivity Analysis of the Effect of Fiscal and Monetary Policy on the Size Distribution of Income in the U.S.," *Advances in Econometrics* 5, 97–122.

Sahota, G. (1978). Theories of personal income distribution: a survey. *Journal of Economic Literature*, 16, 1–55.

Salem, A. B. and T. D. Mount (1974). "A Convenient Descriptive Model of Income Distribution: The Gamma Density," *Econometrica* 42, 1115–1127.

Sargent, T. J. and N. Wallace (1981). "Some Unpleasant Monetarist Arithmetic," Federal Reserve Bank of Minneapolis Quarterly Review, 5, 1–17.

Schultz, T. P. (1965). *The Distribution of Personal Income*. Washington: U.S.G.P.O.

Schultz, T. W. (1963). *The Economic Value of Education*. New York: Columbia University Press.

Sen, A. K. (1970). *Collective Choice and Social Welfare*, Oliver and Boyd, Edinburgh.

Sen, A. (1973). *On Economic Inequality.* Oxford University Press.

Sen, A. K. (1974). "Information Bases of Alternative Welfare Approaches," *Journal of Public Economics* 3, 387–403.

Shorrocks, A. F. (1980). "The Class of Additively Decomposable Inequality Measures," *Econometrica* 48, 613–625.

Shorrocks, A. F. (1982). "Inequality Decomposition by Factor Components," *Econometrica* 50, 193–211.

Shorrocks, A. F. (1983). "The Impact of Income Components on the Distribution of Family Income," *Quarterly Journal of Economics* 98, 1311–326.

Sims, Christopher A. (1972). "Money, Income and Causality" AER 62 540–552.

Singh, S. K. and G. S. Maddala (1976). "A Function for the Size Distribution f Incomes," *Econometrica* 44, 963–970.

Slottje, D. J. (1984). "A Measure of Income Inequality Based Upon the Beta Distribution of the Second Kind," *Economics Letters* 15, 369–375.

Slottje, D. J. (1985). Measuring Income Inequality Utilizing a Flexible Functional Form that Allows for Exact Aggregation and Decomposition of Attributes: The Case of the U.S. for the Years 1960, 1970 and 1980 for Various Attributes, Working Paper #8521, Dallas, TX: Southern Methodist University.

Slottje, D. J. (1987). "Relative Price Changes and Inequality in the Size Distribution of Various Components of Income: A Multidimensional Approach," *Journal of Business and Economic Statistics* 5, 19–26.

Stein, Herbert (1969). *The Fiscal Revolution in America.* University of Chicago Press.

Stigler, G. (1954). "History of Empirical Demand Studies," *Journal of Political Economy* 42, 198–233.

Theil, H. (1967). *Economics and Information Theory,* Amsterdam: North Holland Publishing Company.

Theil, H. (1979). "The Measurement of Inequality by Components of Income," *Economics Letters* 2, 197–199.

Thurow, L. L. (1970). "Analyzing the American Income Distribution," *American Economic Review* 60 (Papers and Proceedings), 261–269.

Tinbergen, Jan (1975). *Income Distribution: Analysis and Policies,* Oxford: North-Holland.

White, H. (1980). "Heteroskedasticity—Consistent Covariance Matrix Estimator and a Direct Test for Heteroskedasticity," *Econometrica* 48, 817–838.

# Author Index

189